IMPERIAL W
MUSEUM

the **D-DAY** EXPERIENCE

from the **INVASION**
to the **LIBERATION** of **PARIS**

Richard **HOLMES**

CARLTON

CONTENTS

Tuesday
6
JUNE
D-DAY

JUNE 1944

FOR EXTERNAL USE ONLY
5 Grams Crystalline
SULFANILAMIDE
H. W. & D.

DIRECTIONS:
Sprinkle evenly over wound
before applying First Aid dressing

Tested and subdivided by
Henson, Westcott & Dunning, Inc.
    Baltimore, Md.

OPEN PULL-UP
AND TEAR OFF
RED FLAP

AIRBORNE

INTRODUCTION

D-DAY IS A LANDMARK IN HISTORY.

It was the largest-ever amphibious operation, and is one of those events for which the much-misused phrase "turning point" is indeed appropriate. Yet there is more to the summer of 1944 than D-Day, crucial though it was. First, we must acknowledge the role played by Russia in eating the heart out of the German army. D-Day is seen in its proper context only if set alongside the Russian Belorussian offensive, which destroyed German Army Group Centre on the Eastern Front that summer.

Second, D-Day was made possible by the Western Allies' efforts elsewhere. Strategic bombing weakened the German industrial base and diverted resources to the defence of the Reich. The long and painful slog up Italy by the men nicknamed "D-Day dodgers" forced the Germans to commit troops who would have been valuable on the Eastern or Western fronts. Nor should we forget that while D-Day was the much-publicized beginning of the end of the war in Europe, in Burma Bill Slim's 14th Army battled on far from the spotlight.

D-Day also relied on naval superiority, so long and so bitterly fought for. Without the Battle of the Atlantic there could have been no D-Day. Though the emphasis of this book is on land operations in France, no historian can be unaware of the part played by the naval plan, Operation Neptune, in enabling the landings to take place in the first instance. Almost 7,000 vessels, from battleships to landing craft, were assigned to Operation Neptune. Most were British, American and Canadian, but it is an indication of the breadth of the coalition that there were French, Norwegian, Dutch, Polish and Greek vessels too.

Last, D-Day's importance all too often obscures the significance of the Normandy campaign as a whole. Getting ashore was only part of the challenge, though challenge it certainly was. The force disembarked in Normandy had to be sustained with food, ammunition and reinforcements along sea lanes kept open by Allied navies, and supported by aircraft from strategic bombers to those ubiquitous Dakotas which helped revolutionize the evacuation of casualties. Many Normandy veterans recall not the landing itself, but the fighting that followed as the Allies strengthened the beachhead and then broke out into France. It has become received wisdom that the First World War was a soldier's war in a way that the Second was not. But there was nothing easy in being an infantryman or tank crewman in Normandy, some of whose battles – like Operation Epsom for the British or the push through the bocage for the Americans – were attritional grinds which would have been familiar to an earlier generation of fighting men.

This is a book that looks at the campaign as a whole, from the beginning of Allied planning to the liberation of Paris. Using the collections of the Imperial War Museum and other institutions, I have tried to produce something that reflects the true texture of the campaign, from German situation maps which show how successful the Allied deception plan actually was, to the log book of an RAF Typhoon pilot. These gems of memorabilia, as fresh today as they were in 1944, set this book apart from the scholarly assessments and popular surveys which rise to greet each D-Day anniversary. I hope that when readers handle this primary material, so carefully reproduced here, they will see the events of that long and bloody summer as something more than history.

I have been a military historian most of my working life, and am increasingly conscious of the way time spins me down its tunnel. When I first visited the battlefields of 1914–18, I was closer in time to them then than I am to Normandy now. When I first visited the D-Day beaches, most of the veterans I met on them were younger than I am now. There will be fewer veterans in Normandy this year, and fewer still next. Yet they lie at the very heart of my story. I grew up in the shadow of the Second World War, and take the view that it was not a struggle from which my father's generation could stand aside. It could, in common with most wars, have been foreseen with greater prescience, and prosecuted with greater efficiency. But my generation owes a lasting debt to the men and women whose sacrifices made Allied victory possible: this book, above all, is their story.

RICHARD HOLMES

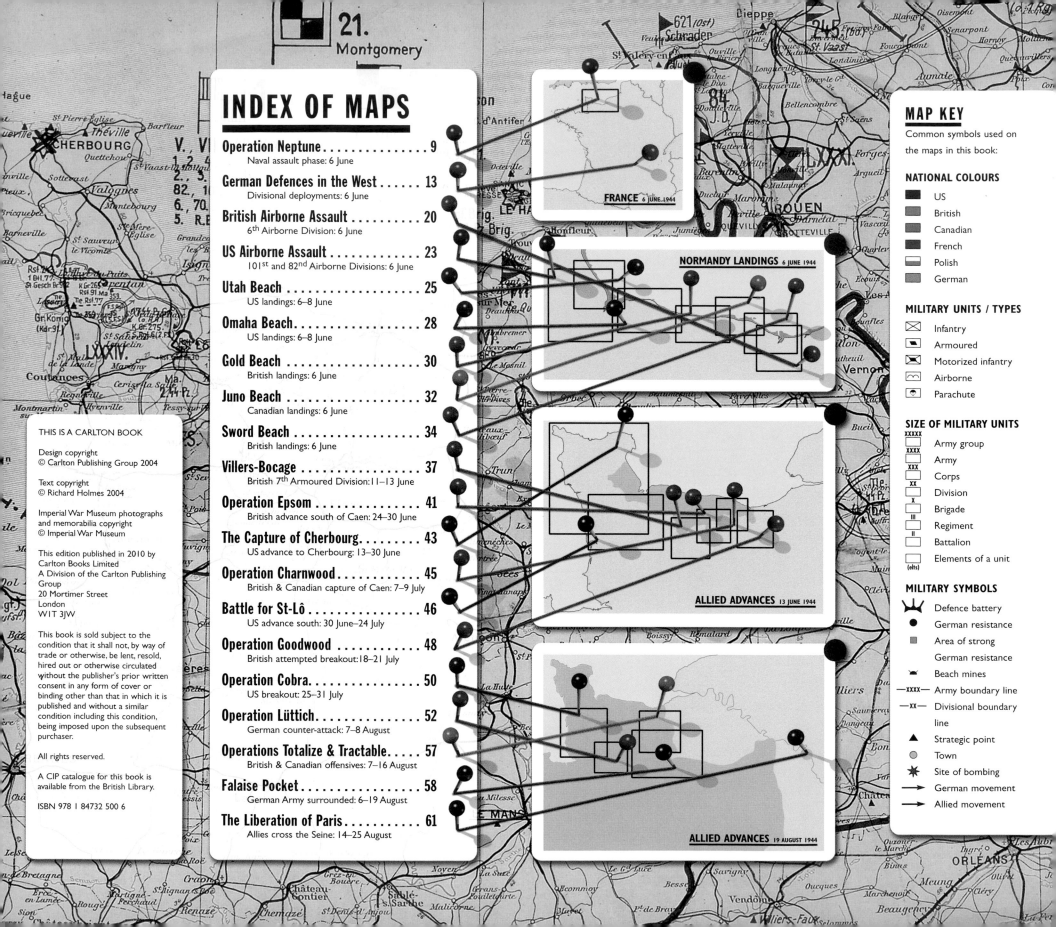

21. Montgomery

INDEX OF MAPS

THIS IS A CARLTON BOOK

Design copyright
© Carlton Publishing Group 2004

Text copyright
© Richard Holmes 2004

Imperial War Museum photographs
and memorabilia copyright
© Imperial War Museum

This edition published in 2010 by
Carlton Books Limited
A Division of the Carlton Publishing
Group
20 Mortimer Street
London
W1T 3JW

A CIP catalogue for this book is
available from the British Library.

ISBN 978 1 84732 500 6

MAP KEY

Common symbols used on
the maps in this book:

NATIONAL COLOURS

US
British
Canadian
French
Polish
German

MILITARY UNITS / TYPES

Infantry
Armoured
Motorized infantry
Airborne
Parachute

SIZE OF MILITARY UNITS

XXXXX Army group
XXXX Army
XXX Corps
XX Division
X Brigade
III Regiment
II Battalion
(elts) Elements of a unit

MILITARY SYMBOLS

Defence battery
German resistance
Area of strong
German resistance
Beach mines
—XXXX— Army boundary line
—XX— Divisional boundary
line
Strategic point
Town
Site of bombing
German movement
Allied movement

THE NORMANDY CAMPAIGN
Allied Advances 6 June—19 August 1944

XXXXX
21 MONTGOMERY

XXXX
BRADLEY

XXXX
2 DEMPSEY

XXX COLLINS

XXX GEROW

XXX 30 RITCHIE

XXX 1 CROKER

XX 4

II Ranger

XX 29

XX 1

XX 50

XX 3 CDN

XX 3

XX 101

XX 82

MAP p.43: CHERBOURG
MAP p.25: UTAH BEACH
MAP p.23: US AIRBORNE ASSAULT
MAP p.28: OMAHA BEACH
MAP p.30: GOLD BEACH
MAP p.32: JUNO BEACH
MAP p.34: SWORD BEACH
MAP p.20: BRITISH AIRBORNE ASSAULT
MAP p.45: CHARNWOOD
MAP p.46: ST-LO
MAP p.41: EPSOM
MAP p.48: GOODWOOD
MAP p.37: VILLERS-BOCAGE
MAP p.50: COBRA
MAP p.57: TOTALIZE & TRACTABLE
MAP p.58: THE FALAISE POCKET
MAP p.52: LUTTICH

German Pocket

0   10 km
0   10 miles

N

Baie de la Seine

CHERBOURG
St-Pierre-Église
Barfleur
Étretat
St-Vaast-la-Hougue
Quettehou
Valognes
Quinéville
Montebourg
Bricquebec
Ravenoville
St-Germain-de-Varreville
St-Martin-de-Varreville
Utah
Ste-Mère-Église
les Pieux
Carteret
Barneville
St-Sauveur-le-Vicomte
Bouteville
Pont-l'Abbé
Beuzeville-la-Bastille
Chef-du-Pont
Vierville
Portbail
Beuzeville-la-Bastille
Ste-Marie-du-Mont
St-Côme-du-Mont
Pointe du Hoc
Omaha
Gold
Juno
Sword
LE HAVRE
Montivilliers
Honfleur
Isigny-sur-Mer
Carentan
Port-en-Bessin
Arromanches
Courseulles-sur-Mer
Langrune-sur-Mer
la Haye-du-Puits
St-Jores
Bayeux
St-Léger
Creully
Riva-Bella
Ouistreham
Cabourg
Houlgate
Trouville-sur-Mer
Deauville
Villers-sur-Mer
Beaumont-en-Auge
Pont-l'Évêque
Lessay
Périers
Ballroy
Tilly-sur-Seulles
Carpiquet
CAEN
Troarn
Dozulé
Lisieux
St-Lô
Caumont-l'Éventé
Villers-Bocage
Bourguébus
Vimont
Crèvecoeur-en-Auge
Coutances
Torigni-sur-Vire
Laize-la-Ville
St-Pierre-sur-Dives
Aunay-sur-Odon
Tessy-sur-Vire
le-Bény-Bocage
Mt. Piçon
Thury-Harcourt
Hill 145
Potigny
Livarot
Bréhal
Gavray
Montchamp
Clécy
Falaise
Vimoutiers
Granville
St-Pair-sur-Mer
Estry
Condé-sur-Noireau
Vassy
la-Haye-Pesnel
Carolles
Sartilly
Vire
St-Sever Calvados
Valedieu-les-Poêles
St-Pois
Tinchebray
Flers
Putanges
Argentan
Écouché
le-Bourg-St-Léonard
Gacé
Avranches
Brécey
Juvigny-le-Terre
Mortain
Sourdeval
Briouze
Rânes
Nonant-le-Pin
Baie du Mont-St-Michel
le Mont-St-Michel
Reffuveille
Ducey
Mortrée

30 JUNE
6 JUNE
31 JULY
19 AUGUST

THE PLANNING

On 12 February 1944 General Dwight D. Eisenhower, Supreme Commander, Allied Expeditionary Force, was directed to "enter the Continent of Europe and, in conjunction with other United Nations, undertake operations aimed at the heart of Germany and the destruction of her armed forces." It had been clear from December 1941 that the defeat of Germany was the principal Allied war aim, although there were many challenges to be overcome before an invasion of Europe could be mounted. War industry had to be developed, and sea and air communications maintained: winning the Battle of the Atlantic against German submarines was to prove crucial. Germany was worn down by land, air and sea, with her industrial capacity eroded by the growing weight of Allied strategic bombing. The war against Japan compelled America and, to a lesser degree, Britain, to devote resources to the Far East, and the relationship with Russia, whose leader Joseph Stalin repeatedly demanded the opening of a second front, had to be developed.

While the Allies were united in their opposition to Germany, they had practical and cultural differences. The British sometimes struck the Americans as over-cautious and preoccupied with imperial concerns, while the Americans sometimes seemed brash and headstrong. Nevertheless, there were sufficient good working relationships within the alliance, notably that between US President Franklin D. Roosevelt and British Prime Minister Winston Churchill, to ensure that strategy moved inexorably in the right direction.

Operation Bolero saw the concentration of US men and equipment in Britain. After the Allied invasion of North Africa in November 1942, an Allied conference at Casablanca outlined plans for the invasion of Europe in 1944. Although a Supreme Allied Commander was not yet nominated, the British Lieutenant General F. E. Morgan was appointed "Chief of Staff to the Supreme Allied Commander (designate)", Cossac for short. The Washington conference in May 1943 elaborated the forces that he would have at his disposal, and ordered that a draft of the plan for what was now called Operation Overlord should be ready by 1 August. The planners were helped by the fact that much work had already been done on similar projects. Combined Operations Headquarters had played a key role in pulling together tri-service experience.

NAVAL FORCES ASSIGNED TO OPERATION NEPTUNE (THE NAVAL ASSAULT PHASE)

NAVAL COMBATANT VESSELS:	1,213
LANDING SHIPS AND CRAFT:	4,126
ANCILLARY SHIPS AND CRAFT:	736
MERCHANT SHIPS:	864
TOTAL:	**6,939**
BRITISH/CANADIAN:	79%
US:	16.5%
OTHER ALLIES:	4.5%

133,000 MEN LANDED FROM THE SEA

RIGHT *The insignia of the Supreme Headquarters Allied Expeditionary Forces (SHAEF). The flaming sword represents avenging Allied forces; the black, the darkness of Nazism; and the rainbow, the liberty to come.*

ABOVE *Envelope used for circulating SHAEF meeting minutes.*

ABOVE *After the raid: Dieppe, 19 August 1942, where 2nd Canadian Infantry Division suffered over 3,300 casualties. Fire support was hopelessly inadequate, and planners had not assessed the effect of shingle on tank tracks.*

LEFT *Band of Brothers? The Allied commanders, 1 February 1944. From left to right: Bradley, Ramsay, Tedder, Eisenhower, Montgomery, Leigh-Mallory, and Eisenhower's chief of staff, Walter Bedell Smith.*

RIGHT *A Sicilian beach seen from a British landing craft. Two Allied armies invaded Sicily in July 1943. The amphibious landings went comparatively well, but airborne operations were marred by poor weather.*

The Dieppe raid of August 1942, when a Canadian division had been landed with disastrous results, was amongst the landings from which planners could draw lessons.

The Cossac team considered three invasion areas: the Pas de Calais, Normandy and Brittany. The latter was ruled out by distance, both from Britain and from Allied objectives in Europe, and the Pas de Calais was too obvious. It was decided that Normandy, with its large port at Cherbourg, was a better choice.

The outline plan envisaged an amphibious assault by three divisions, with airborne divisions dropped on both flanks. There were still unanswered questions, notably who would actually command the invasion, and how

enough landing craft could be made available. But in December 1943 it was announced that Eisenhower would take command, with Air Chief Marshal Sir Arthur Tedder as his deputy. All three component commanders were British: General Sir Bernard Montgomery would command ground forces, Admiral Sir Bertram Ramsay naval forces, and Air Chief Marshal Sir Trafford Leigh-Mallory air forces. Montgomery recognized that the blow delivered by the Cossac plan was unlikely to be sufficiently heavy, and in early 1944 he expanded it to comprise an amphibious assault by five divisions with drops by three airborne divisions.

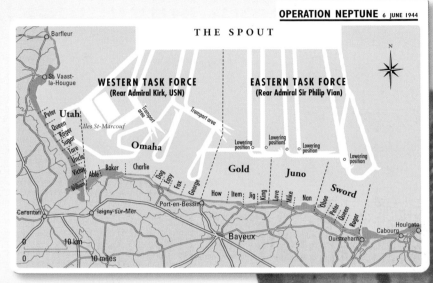

OPERATION NEPTUNE 6 JUNE 1944

THE SPOUT

WESTERN TASK FORCE
(Rear Admiral Kirk, USN)

EASTERN TASK FORCE
(Rear Admiral Sir Philip Vian)

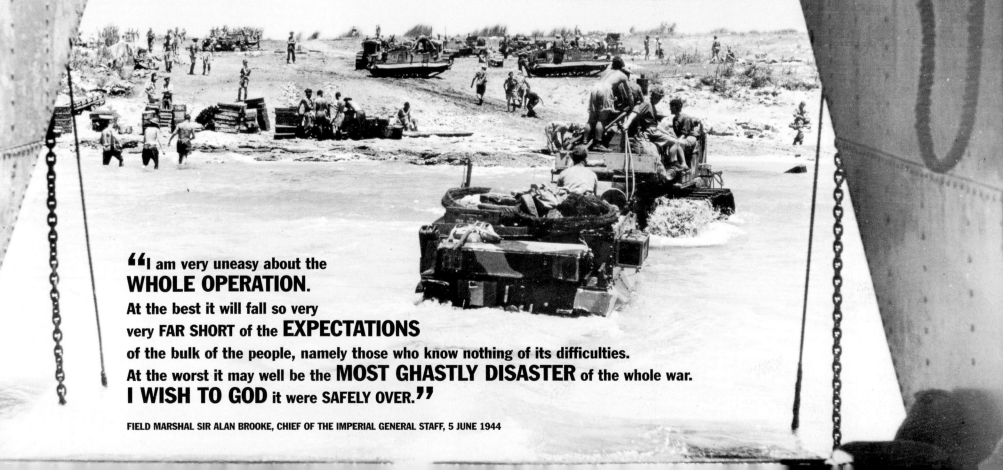

"I am very uneasy about the WHOLE OPERATION. At the best it will fall so very very FAR SHORT of the EXPECTATIONS of the bulk of the people, namely those who know nothing of its difficulties. At the worst it may well be the MOST GHASTLY DISASTER of the whole war. I WISH TO GOD it were SAFELY OVER."

FIELD MARSHAL SIR ALAN BROOKE, CHIEF OF THE IMPERIAL GENERAL STAFF, 5 JUNE 1944

THE LEADERS

The leaders of the forces that clashed in Normandy presented a sharp contrast. Dwight Eisenhower, born in 1890, the son of a railway worker, was commissioned in 1913. He saw no action in the First World War, but worked closely with US Army Chief of Staff George C. Marshall and, although decidedly junior, commanded the North African landings in 1942. Eisenhower emerged as a skilful conciliator rather than a flamboyant leader. He had deep reserves of moral courage, and though he can be criticized for spending too long looking up to the military/political level rather than down to the operational/tactical level, his common sense and good nature were invaluable strengths. While Tedder, his British deputy, was devoted to him, the prickly but experienced Montgomery argued that Eisenhower had no real grasp of his task. Ramsay was a hard-working and level-headed naval officer who did much to make Operation Neptune, the naval part of the invasion plan, work well. Leigh-Mallory was an experienced fighter commander, on poor terms with the "bomber barons" whose heavy aircraft froze off the invasion sector. He got on badly with both Coningham, whose Allied Second Tactical Air Force provided air cover in Normandy, and Montgomery, who thought him over-cautious.

The German Commander in Chief West was Field Marshal Gerd von Rundstedt. Born in 1875, Rundstedt served throughout the First World War, retired on age grounds in 1938, but commanded army groups in 1940 and 1941. He was brought back from retirement to be Commander in Chief West in March 1942. Rundstedt was brave, honourable and conventional. He did not enjoy Eisenhower's power, for neither German air nor naval forces in the west (small though both were) answered to him, and his authority was so circumscribed by Hitler that he quipped that the only troops he could move were the sentries at his gates. Rundstedt clashed with Field Marshal Erwin

LEFT *Leigh-Mallory, a First World War pilot, played a prominent part in the Battle of Britain, and headed Fighter Command from 1942. His tenure as Eisenhower's air commander was marred by personality clashes.*

Rommel, whose Army Group B held the invasion area. Rommel, his reputation made in North Africa, threw his energy into the improvement of beach defences. He argued that the invasion had to be stopped on the beaches, so German armour must be committed early. His experience convinced him that the traditional solution of identifying the main thrust and concentrating to meet it would not work in the face of Allied air power. Hitler imposed a compromise solution which was to leave the armoured divisions of Panzer Group West too far from the coast, and only a single armoured division, 21st Panzer, came into action on D-Day.

The Allies enjoyed advantages before the first shot was fired. Although there was some friction in their chain of command, the structure was logical, and the supreme commander had the temperament for his task. The German system, in contrast, mirrored the conflicting power blocs of the Third Reich, with the heavy hand of Hitler all too apparent.

ABOVE *Although Eisenhower lacked great operational experience, his engaging manner and easy style made him a natural coalition commander.*

21st ARMY GROUP

ABOVE *Ramsay had retired from the navy before the war, but was the directing brain of the Dunkirk evacuation in 1940. He made a characteristically level-headed contribution to Allied planning in 1944.*

RIGHT *Tedder had commanded the Mediterranean Allied Air Forces before being appointed Eisenhower's deputy. He was a staunch supporter of Ike's, but had little time for Montgomery.*

ABOVE *Early in 1944 Montgomery was given command of 21st Army Group comprising all Allied land forces committed to D-Day.*

ALLIED CHAIN OF COMMAND
NORMANDY, 6 JUNE 1944

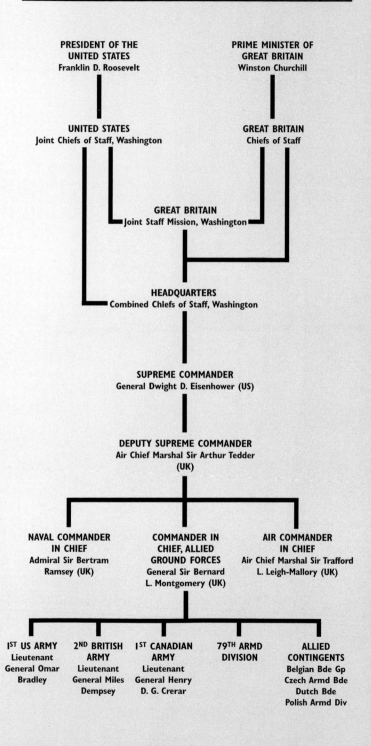

PRESIDENT OF THE UNITED STATES
Franklin D. Roosevelt

PRIME MINISTER OF GREAT BRITAIN
Winston Churchill

UNITED STATES
Joint Chiefs of Staff, Washington

GREAT BRITAIN
Chiefs of Staff

GREAT BRITAIN
Joint Staff Mission, Washington

HEADQUARTERS
Combined Chiefs of Staff, Washington

SUPREME COMMANDER
General Dwight D. Eisenhower (US)

DEPUTY SUPREME COMMANDER
Air Chief Marshal Sir Arthur Tedder (UK)

NAVAL COMMANDER IN CHIEF
Admiral Sir Bertram Ramsey (UK)

COMMANDER IN CHIEF, ALLIED GROUND FORCES
General Sir Bernard L. Montgomery (UK)

AIR COMMANDER IN CHIEF
Air Chief Marshal Sir Trafford L. Leigh-Mallory (UK)

1ST US ARMY
Lieutenant General Omar Bradley

2ND BRITISH ARMY
Lieutenant General Miles Dempsey

1ST CANADIAN ARMY
Lieutenant General Henry D. G. Crerar

79TH ARMD DIVISION

ALLIED CONTINGENTS
Belgian Bde Gp
Czech Armd Bde
Dutch Bde
Polish Armd Div

GERMAN CHAIN OF COMMAND
NORMANDY, 6 JUNE 1944

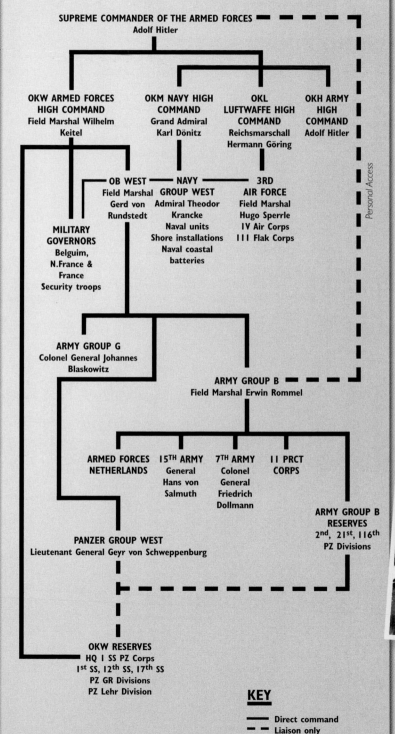

SUPREME COMMANDER OF THE ARMED FORCES
Adolf Hitler

OKW ARMED FORCES HIGH COMMAND
Field Marshal Wilhelm Keitel

OKM NAVY HIGH COMMAND
Grand Admiral Karl Dönitz

OKL LUFTWAFFE HIGH COMMAND
Reichsmarschall Hermann Göring

OKH ARMY HIGH COMMAND
Adolf Hitler

OB WEST
Field Marshal Gerd von Rundstedt

NAVY GROUP WEST
Admiral Theodor Krancke
Naval units
Shore installations
Naval coastal batteries

3RD AIR FORCE
Field Marshal Hugo Sperrle
IV Air Corps
III Flak Corps

MILITARY GOVERNORS
Belguim, N.France & France
Security troops

ARMY GROUP G
Colonel General Johannes Blaskowitz

ARMY GROUP B
Field Marshal Erwin Rommel

ARMED FORCES NETHERLANDS

15TH ARMY
General Hans von Salmuth

7TH ARMY
Colonel General Friedrich Dollmann

II PRCT CORPS

ARMY GROUP B RESERVES
2nd, 21st, 116th PZ Divisions

PANZER GROUP WEST
Lieutenant General Geyr von Schweppenburg

OKW RESERVES
HQ I SS PZ Corps
1st SS, 12th SS, 17th SS
PZ GR Divisions
PZ Lehr Division

Personal Access

KEY

— Direct command
- - - Liaison only

ABOVE *Rundstedt, born in 1875, had actually retired in 1938, but commanded army groups in 1940 and 1941. After another spell of retirement he became Commander in Chief West in 1942.*

ABOVE *Rommel had an outstanding First World War record as an infantry officer, and was a divisional commander in 1940. He shot to prominence as commander of Axis troops in North Africa.*

GERMAN FORCES & DEFENCES

BELOW *This propaganda shot shows a fast-firing MG 34 machine gun in a beach bunker. The soldier on the right has two stick grenades to hand.*

RIGHT *Identity disk of one of the Organization Todt construction workers. The disk was discovered in 1988 on the site of a POW camp for Germans at Foucarville, behind Utah Beach. In the spring of 1944 Organization Todt, under the direction of Albert Speer, had committed around 18,000 men to Atlantic Wall building duties.*

FRIEDRICH DOLLMANN

was commissioned into the Bavarian field artillery in 1901 and spent the First World War in regimental and staff appointments. He commanded 7th Army in the 1940 campaign, earning the Knight's Cross and promotion to colonel general. Dollmann remained in the same post, and by 1944 lacked any recent combat experience. Criticized by Hitler for permitting the fall of Cherbourg, Dollmann probably committed suicide at Le Mans on 28 June, though formal records attribute his death to a heart attack.

For the Germans, the west was "a poor man's war" overshadowed by the struggle against the Russians. Rundstedt was responsible for the whole of France and the Low Countries, with 1st and 19th Armies of Army Group G covering the area south of the Loire, 7th and 15th Armies of Army Group B dealing with the Loire to the Dutch border, and Armed Forces Netherlands holding Holland. He had to do much with little. General Blumentritt, his chief of staff, complained that there was insufficient motor transport: infantry divisions had to rely on horses. Air attacks had reduced the flow of fuel, ammunition and spares, and many units had to detrain so far back that they were already tired by the time they came into battle. Some formations, like the SS Panzer divisions, were very good indeed, but others had been worn down by combat in the east and had not yet been fully reconstituted. Coastal divisions had weak artillery and little inherent mobility. Many of their officers and men had already been wounded, and one division was composed entirely of men with stomach ailments. The Germans made wide use of *Osttruppen*, recruited from amongst Russian prisoners of war and comprising a variety of national and ethnic groups: there were no less than 21 "Russian" battalions in the 7th Army alone. Blumentritt identified 25 different types of division which varied in composition, with requirements for spares and ammunition which made them a quartermaster's nightmare.

Although the Germans were certain that the Allies would indeed invade – in November 1943 Hitler issued a directive foreseeing an offensive "not later than the spring, perhaps earlier" – they were unsure as to time and place. Most generals, deciding on the basis of traditional military education, thought the Pas de Calais, the most direct route, a more likely objective than Normandy. Hitler, reasoning intuitively, suspected that Normandy was more probable, but General Walter Warlimont admitted that his comrades were "not quite convinced" by this. The Germans were in a state of acute air inferiority, although many generals argued that this had less effect on the outcome of individual battles than it did on movement behind the lines. "It was like pitting a racehorse against a motor car," wrote one.

Yet it was not that simple. The Germans had some first-rate weapons, like the 88mm anti-tank gun, and tanks like the Panther and Tiger. Until defeats in the east and west in mid-1944 struck fatal damage to its replacement system, the German army took more time and trouble to train senior NCOs than the British and Americans took to train junior officers. And if the fighting on the Eastern Front had done terrible damage to the Germans, it had also left them with a hard-forged nucleus of experienced junior commanders, men like Michael Wittmann, who almost single-handedly stopped the British 7th Armoured Division on 14 June, and Hans von Luck, whose determination did so much to thwart British plans in Operation Goodwood the following month. Allied policy of offering Germany only unconditional surrender persuaded many German soldiers, even if they had little sympathy with the Nazis, that failure in Normandy would result in the invasion of their homeland. The defenders of Normandy were certainly not supermen: but this was an army with proud traditions, fighting with its back to the wall against adversaries who enjoyed quantitative superiority but often lacked experience and the sheer killer instinct.

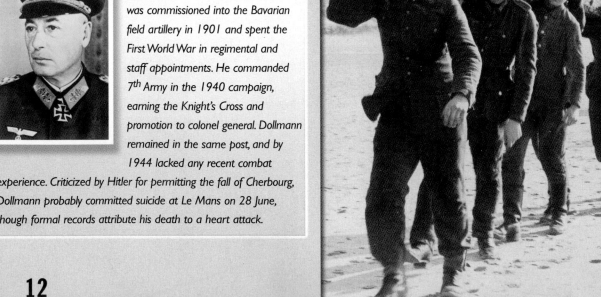

LEFT *A 1943 German photograph shows the erection of beach defences. These anti-landing obstacles were primitive by the standards of the Atlantic Wall in June 1944.*

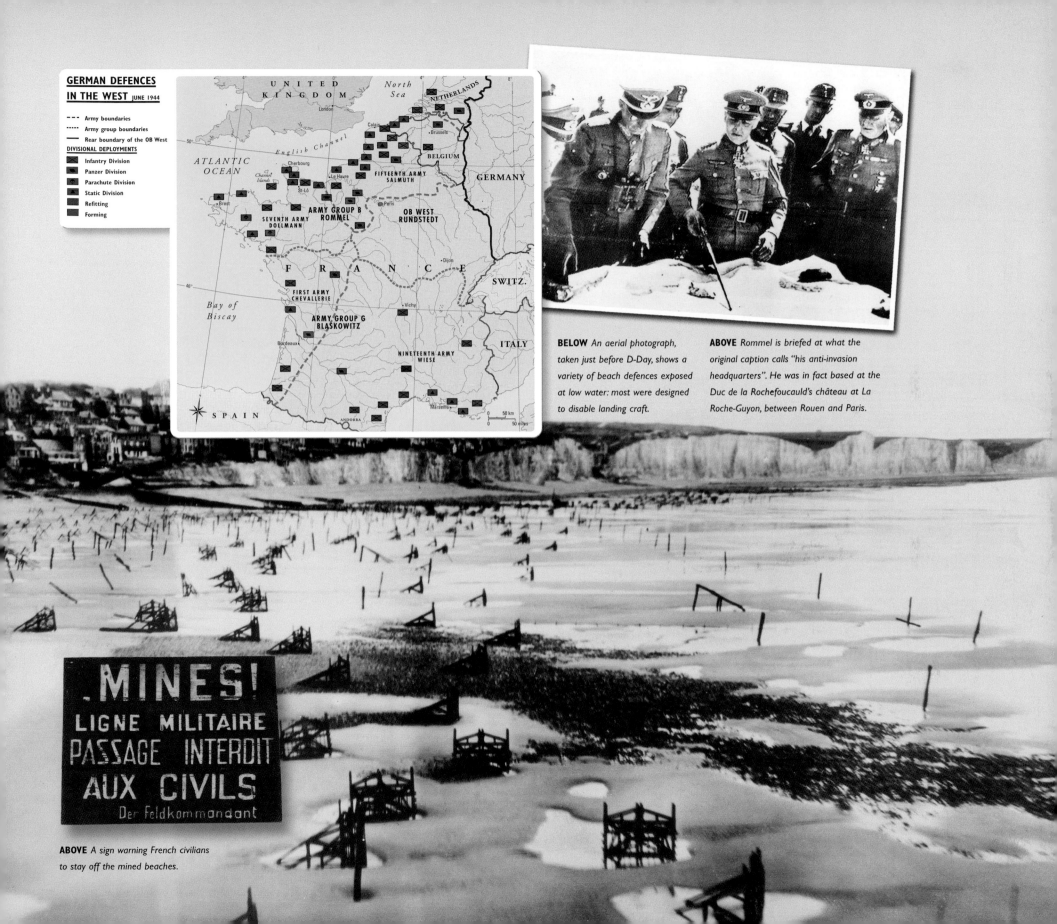

GERMAN DEFENCES IN THE WEST JUNE 1944

- - - Army boundaries
······ Army group boundaries
——— Rear boundary of the OB West

DIVISIONAL DEPLOYMENTS

Infantry Division
Panzer Division
Parachute Division
Static Division
Refitting
Forming

BELOW An aerial photograph, taken just before D-Day, shows a variety of beach defences exposed at low water: most were designed to disable landing craft.

ABOVE Rommel is briefed at what the original caption calls "his anti-invasion headquarters". He was in fact based at the Duc de la Rochefoucauld's château at La Roche-Guyon, between Rouen and Paris.

MINES!
LIGNE MILITAIRE
PASSAGE INTERDIT
AUX CIVILS
Der Feldkommandant

ABOVE A sign warning French civilians to stay off the mined beaches.

DECEPTION & INTELLIGENCE

BELOW *The 25-pound field gun was the workhorse of British artillery. This dummy gun, limber and truck, intended to deceive an observer from 500–1,000 yards, were collapsible and folded flat for stowage.*

If the Germans had obtained timely and accurate information they could have stopped the invasion in its tracks: intelligence and deception were fundamental to the campaign's outcome. The Allies had to glean information on a wide range of factors, to keep their own preparations secret and to persuade the Germans that the invasion would take place elsewhere.

The British had penetrated German ciphers to produce invaluable signals intelligence known as Ultra (short for Top Secret Ultra). They had also cracked the Japanese diplomatic cipher, so that reports sent from Berlin to Tokyo fell into their hands. And while German agents in Britain had fared badly, the double agent Garbo (a Spaniard called Juan Pajol) fed the Germans a rich diet of misinformation, helping convince them that the Normandy landings were one part of a two-pronged thrust, with the second aimed at the Pas de Calais.

Operation Fortitude relayed the same message on a larger scale. A fictitious First US Army Group (FUSAG) was "stationed" in south-east England, and fake camps and spurious radio traffic were designed to persuade the Germans that substantial forces were ready for the short hop across the Channel. Fortitude North produced a fictitious 4th Army in Scotland, ready to invade Norway. German intelligence, like the chain of command in Normandy, lacked a single controlling voice, and its various agencies "vied with each other in supplying Hitler with reports."

Allied intelligence on Normandy came from many sources. The BBC appealed for holiday postcards of the whole of France, and relevant ones were collated. The French Resistance produced information on German defences and deployments. Some air photographs revealed the landscape from above, while others, taken from low-flying aircraft, helped create the beach panorama which would be visible from landing craft. Although the Allied air forces softened up objectives in Normandy, more bombs were dropped outside the invasion sector than within it. Experts made night-time landings on Normandy beaches to take sand samples which would help ascertain their load-bearing capacity. By the time D-Day arrived the Allies enjoyed excellent intelligence, while their opponents were shrouded by the fog of war.

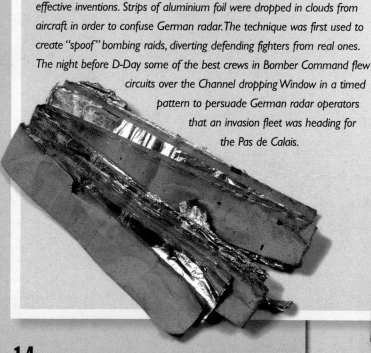

WINDOW *was the codename for one of the war's simplest but most effective inventions. Strips of aluminium foil were dropped in clouds from aircraft in order to confuse German radar. The technique was first used to create "spoof" bombing raids, diverting defending fighters from real ones. The night before D-Day some of the best crews in Bomber Command flew circuits over the Channel dropping Window in a timed pattern to persuade German radar operators that an invasion fleet was heading for the Pas de Calais.*

ABOVE *This pneumatic dummy Sherman tank, made by Dunlop Rubber Company, could be blown up like a balloon.*

ABOVE *When deflated, the dummy Sherman tank fitted into a valise only slightly larger than a sports bag.*

RIGHT *These full-sized dummy Landing Craft, Tanks (LCT), each 160 feet long, were used in harbours in south-east England to suggest that the invasion would be directed at the Pas de Calais.*

"GENFLDM VON RUNSDTEDT and his staff expected the INVASION ... somewhere between Calais and the mouth of the Seine. This was the most VULNERABLE AREA for the shortest thrust through NORTHERN FRANCE AND BELGIUM into GERMANY and the RUHR."

GENERAL GUNTHER BLUMENTRITT, CHIEF OF STAFF, COMMANDER IN CHIEF WEST

THE RESISTANCE & SOE

RIGHT Crève-pneus – a box of mines used by the French Resistance for blowing up the tyres of German vehicles. No identifying marks of any kind were used on equipment dropped by the Allies for use by the Resistance.

BELOW
Resistance groups used weapons parachuted in by the Allies or captured from the Germans. This truck bears the Cross of Lorraine, and FFI for Forces Françaises de l'Intérieur.

German victory in 1940 divided France. There were those who agreed with Marshal Pétain, head of the new French state based at the spa town of Vichy, that defeat was the outcome of decadence. And there were others who believed in armed resistance. There were some stirrings early on, and the German invasion of Russia in 1941 brought French Communists into the struggle. However, the Resistance grew gradually, and was marked by the factionalism which mirrored French politics.

In 1940 the Special Operations Executive (SOE) was set up "to co-ordinate all action, by way of subversion and sabotage, against the enemy overseas…." It was divided into "country sections", though France was the responsibility of several sections. Section RF worked with General de Gaulle's Free French in London, but Section F did not, and SOE's historian observes that inter-section jealousies "often raged with virulence." The US equivalent of SOE, the Office of Strategic Services (OSS) also maintained a French section.

SOE recruited men and women from a cross-section of British and French society. A young peer was killed in Normandy in 1942; a successful sabotage team was led by a fireman and a garage hand. Agents were sent to France by parachute or Westland Lysander light aircraft. They carried out numerous tasks, from sabotage of key installations, through the collection of intelligence to the organization of arms drops. If captured they could expect no mercy. As their historian wrote: "The best died silent; or if they had to talk, said nothing the enemy wanted to hear."

Resistance groups made a major contribution to the Allied war effort in 1944, by providing intelligence on defences (one bicycle-racer from Bayeux regularly sped along the coast road with plans concealed in his handle-bars) and by the methodical sabotage of rail and telephone communications. In March 1944 de Gaulle decreed that the Resistance would be assimilated into the French army as the Forces Françaises de l'Intérieur, but Communist FTP groups generally declined to obey. Although the importance of the Resistance was later exaggerated, it was important both for its practical work and for the way it kept the soul of France alive.

ABOVE In an image replete with symbolism, local people inspect a multi-barelled **Nebelwerfer** (Moaning Minnie to Allied soldiers) captured at Fleury-sur-Orne. The bunker behind sheltered villagers during the subsequent fighting.

RIGHT Heavy bombers of the US 8th Air Force, based in Britain, dropping weapons and equipment to the Resistance in 1944.

VIOLETTE SZABO

was the spirited daughter of an English father and French mother who married a Free French officer in 1940. She joined SOE in 1943, and was parachuted into France on a reconnaissance mission in April 1944. Recovered by a Lysander light aircraft, she was parachuted into Limoges 24 hours after D-Day to help co-ordinate Resistance work with the Allied invasion. However, she encountered a German patrol and was captured when her ammunition ran out. Subsequently shot in Ravensbruck concentration camp, she was awarded a posthumous George Cross, Britain's supreme award for gallantry off the field of battle.

ABOVE The Resistance made a valuable contribution to the "War of the Rails". This railway depot on the German lines of communication was sabotaged in March 1944.

Railway-track bomb detonator used by the French Resistance in Normandy. Disruption of the railway network played an important part in reducing the flow of German reinforcements to the invasion area.

17

PEGASUS BRIDGE

The bridges over the Caen Canal and the River Orne – the former codenamed Pegasus and the latter Horsa – provided a crucial link between invasion beaches and airborne landings. In British hands, they would enable armour landed by sea to operate east of the river. Held by the Germans, they might form a barrier between sea-landed and airborne forces, or enable German tanks to take the landings in the flank.

They would be seized by glider assault by Major John Howard's D Company, 2nd Battalion The Oxfordshire and Buckinghamshire Light Infantry. Howard had been a regular army NCO before the war, and was an Oxford policeman in 1939. Having rejoined the army, he was commissioned in 1940. He commanded a tough company, and placed special emphasis on night training. Howard had three platoons, and was reinforced by two more, and a troop of engineers. The force would land in six Horsa gliders, three for each bridge, with Howard leading the assault on Pegasus and Captain Brian Priday that on Horsa. The company had a close relationship with its pilots. When aerial photographs revealed that the Germans were digging holes for anti-glider poles, Staff Sergeant Jim Wallwork, Howard's pilot, told the men that even if the poles were in place they would help by slowing down the overloaded gliders.

Wallwork took off from Tarrant Rushton at 10.56 pm on 5 June, and landed near the eastern end of Pegasus just after midnight. One man was killed in the landing, but within minutes Howard's team had secured the bridge, only Lieutenant Den Brotheridge being killed. Although the troops attacking Horsa landed further from it, their assault was also successful, and Howard ordered his radio operator to send the success signal, "Ham and Jam". There were sporadic German probes during the night and the following morning, but not the armoured counter-attack that the British feared. Howard's men were reinforced by paras during the night and at about 1.00 pm on 6 June they heard bagpipes heralding the approach of Lord Lovat's 1st Special Services Brigade from the beaches. They had taken the bridges as ordered, and held them till relieved.

Tuesday 6 JUNE D-DAY

BRITISH 6TH AIRBORNE DIVISION

TOP LEFT *Number 1 and 2 gliders within yards of Pegasus Bridge. Behind the line of trees the Café Gondrée, the first French building to be liberated on D-Day, is visible across the Caen Canal.*

Major John Howard's hand-drawn sketch showing planned defensive positions for his six glider-borne platoons.

ABOVE *The Colt .45 pistol carried by Captain Vaughan of the Royal Army Medical Corps, who was in glider 3 of Major John Howard's assault force at Pegasus Bridge.*

MACHINE GUN
EMPLACEMENT
x
x BARBED
x WIRE
x
PILLBOX x
(LATER HOWARD'S H.Q.)
x x
x

N

ANTI-TANK
GUN

CANAL DE CAEN

HORSA BRIDGE →

TRENCHES
AND
BUNKERS

①

PEGASUS BRIDGE

GLIDERS

POND

HORSA BRIDGE

②

③

JOHN HOWARD had left the regular army before the war, joining the Oxford police in 1939. Recalled to service, he rose rapidly and received a commission in 1940. His company was specially selected for its D-Day mission, and he was awarded the Distinguished Service Order for his achievement. Slightly wounded, he was more seriously hit later, and was badly injured in a jeep crash that November. A civil servant after the war, he remained a respected figure on veterans' visits to Normandy.

LEFT Major Howard's "Acme Thunderer" whistle, worn round his neck during the assault on Pegasus Bridge, and used to rally his troops in the dark.

ABOVE Aerial reconnaissance photograph showing Pegasus Bridge over the Caen Canal and Horsa Bridge over the Orne River after Major Howard's attack.

LARGE PHOTOGRAPH LEFT Aerial reconnaissance photograph showing the three Horsa gliders of Major John Howard's Pegasus Bridge assault force. Note the broken fuselage of number 2 glider, caused by pilot Oliver Boland's last-minute swerve to avoid hitting the lead glider.

INSET LEFT Allied troops in control of Pegasus Bridge. John Howard's number 1 glider is still visible across the canal.

19

BRITISH AIRBORNE ASSAULT

Tuesday
6
JUNE
D-DAY

BELOW *Shoulder patch and "wings" worn by British glider pilots.*

GLIDER PILOT REGT.

BELOW LEFT *This photograph, taken on 5 June, shows Horsa gliders on the runway with the Halifax bombers which will tow them to France standing ready. All aircraft bear the Allied recognition stripes.*

BELOW RIGHT *The main airborne drop was preceded by the arrival of Pathfinders who set up beacons to mark dropping zones. These Pathfinders are synchronizing their watches before boarding their aircraft.*

The British 6th Airborne Division, commanded by Major General Richard "Windy" Gale, was dropped between the River Orne and the high ground of the Bois de Bavent to secure the eastern flank of the invasion sector. Some of its units had special missions: a reinforced glider company, as we have seen, seized Pegasus Bridge. The 9th Parachute Battalion was to take the German coastal battery at Merville. Its plan was disrupted when some attackers were dropped far away, and although the guns (which proved to be smaller-calibre than had been expected) were put out of action, the battery was briefly reoccupied by the Germans. Men of 3rd Parachute Squadron Royal Engineers were to destroy the bridges over the River Bures so as to prevent the Germans using them. They succeeded in destroying those at Troarn, Bures and Robehomme, and with the assistance of 1st Canadian Parachute Battalion, that over a tributary stream at Varaville.

The division's two parachute brigades, 3rd and

Intended landing zones · Battery destroyed
Actual landing zones · German strongpoints
Bridge captured · German resistance points
Bridge destroyed

RIGHT *An aerial view of 6th Airlanding Brigade's landing zone near Ranville. The high ground of the Bois de Bavent is at the top of the photograph. The gliders remained in situ for weeks to come.*

5th, were dropped during the night, and most units were widely scattered. Many soldiers spent a confusing night endeavouring to link up with their comrades in the darkness, colliding with German patrols and securing strongpoints. One estimate suggests that not more than 60 per cent of the 4,800 men of the division who were landed in France on D-Day were actually able to participate in the day's fighting. On the morning of 6 June, 4th Airlanding Brigade began to arrive by glider, and with it came heavy engineer stores, light tanks and jeeps, field and anti-tank guns, putting the division in a much better position to resist any attack by German armour. It is a measure of the risks run by glider pilots that 71 of the 196 who landed became casualties.

Although the eastern flank was now largely secure it was certainly anything but quiet. The village of Bréville, up on the ridge overlooking the main glider landing zone, was the one hole in the division's perimeter. On the night of 12 June it was attacked by a scratch force based on the much-depleted 12th Parachute Battalion. The two brigadiers involved were wounded, and 12th Parachute Battalion lost 141 of the 160 officers and men who attacked, including the commanding officer. However, by dawn the village was secured, and Major General Gale later declared that its seizure was the turning point in the fight for the Orne bridgehead. It is axiomatic that airborne troops are best used for operations requiring dash, and should be withdrawn as soon as their objectives have been taken. But 6th Airborne Division remained up on the hard shoulder it had created throughout the long and bloody Normandy summer, demonstrating that it could cope with a long attritional slog as well as with the dangerous chaos of an airborne assault.

RIGHT *Two military police NCOs of 6th Airborne Division guard a cross-roads near the village of Ranville on 9 July. There is a Horsa glider in the background.*

RICHARD "WINDY" GALE *commanded 6th Airborne Division in Normandy. Brought up in Australia, he served in the Machine Gun Corps in the First World War, winning the Military Cross, but was only a lieutenant colonel in 1940. Promoted to head Britain's first airborne brigade, he was director of airborne forces at the War Office before taking command of 6th Airborne Division as a major general. After the war he commanded the British Army of the Rhine and served as Deputy Supreme Allied Commander Europe.*

US AIRBORNE ASSAULT

MAXWELL D. TAYLOR

was commissioned from West Point in 1922 but was only a major when war broke out. Quickly promoted, he commanded the artillery of 82nd Airborne Division, and in 1943 carried out a dangerous mission behind the lines in Italy. He led 101st Airborne Division in Normandy and in Operation Market Garden in September. He later served as Chief of Staff of the US Army, Chairman of the Joint Chiefs, and US Ambassador to Vietnam.

US 101ST AIRBORNE DIVISION

RIGHT *Eisenhower had an easy style with soldiers. Here he talks to paratroopers of the 101st Airborne Division at Greenham Common airfield on 5 June 1944. The censor has obscured their divisional flashes.*

RIGHT *A stick of parachutists ready to jump above the Cotentin early on 6 June. The heavily laden men have hooked their static lines, which will open their chutes, onto the cable above them.*

Two US airborne divisions, Major General Matthew B. Ridgway's 82nd and Major General Maxwell Taylor's 101st were to land at the base of the Cotentin peninsula on the western flank of the invasion beaches. Each had two three-battalion parachute infantry regiments and one glider infantry regiment, with supporting artillery and engineers. Some planners favoured a bolder project, the establishment of an airhead in the area of Evreux and Dreux to threaten the Seine crossings and Paris, but Eisenhower, arguing that the force would be vulnerable once it had landed, favoured a more conservative option. However, some argued that the Cotentin plan was risky enough as it stood. Leigh-Mallory called it "a very speculative operation", and had it modified so that many of the gliders would arrive on the evening of D-Day.

It was eventually decided that 101st Airborne Division would be dropped behind Utah Beach, to secure the beach exits and be prepared to exploit through Carentan. 82nd Airborne Division was to land further north-west, astride the River Merderet, to capture the crossings over the river, seize the little town of Ste-Mère-Eglise, on the main Cherbourg-Bayeux road, and be prepared to exploit westwards. The Germans had flooded the valleys, turning the area into a patchwork of inundated fields laced with deeper watercourses and dotted with solidly built Norman villages and farms.

The first wave of parachutists, some 13,000 men, was to be dropped from 822 C-47 aircraft. Many pilots lacked experience for their demanding task, and in the early hours of 6 June this became even more difficult as a bank of thick cloud confronted them as they flew in from the east. A mixture of poor visibility and ground fire scattered the aircraft and, with them, the parachutists they dropped. Some were released too late and fell into the sea, or drowned in flooded rivers: others hit trees or roofs. Most who landed safely were hopelessly lost, and spent the night searching for other Americans, bumping into German patrols, with losses on both sides, or simply sleeping.

MATTHEW B. RIDGWAY

MATTHEW B. RIDGWAY *joined the infantry from West Point in 1917. In 1939 he accompanied US Army Chief of Staff George C. Marshall on a mission to South America. Ridgway commanded 82nd Infantry Division in 1942, supervising its conversion to an airborne formation. After leading his division in Normandy he commanded XVIII Airborne Corps. In 1950 he succeeded Douglas MacArthur at the head of the US Eighth Army in Korea, and was US Army Chief of Staff from 1953–56.*

US 82ND AIRBORNE DIVISION

...the 505th Parachute Infantry Regiment of 82nd Airborne Division was dropped close to Ste-Mère-Eglise; one earlier landed with his parachute hooked onto the town church's steeple and played... but others were less lucky, cut down among the garrison alerted by Allied bombing of the village. The town was secured early on, and the main road was blocked after a spirited action at Neuville. By the end of the day, 82nd Airborne was strongly positioned around Ste-Mère-Eglise, but was in contact neither with the troops coming ashore at Utah Beach nor with the 101st. It had lost over 1,200 men, over half of them missing. Maxwell Taylor's men were more fortunate. Although only about 2,500 of his 6,600 men dropped had assembled by the evening of D-Day, they seized many of their objectives. And secured the exits from Utah Beach and one of the bridges over Carentan.

The dispersal of the drops helped to confuse the German defenders. German commanders spent the early hours trying to build up a picture of reports which gave no clear picture of what had happened. Many were away at a war-game at Rennes. The 91st division's commander, Lieutenant-General Wilhelm Falley, was killed on his way back by a party of paratroops. Like the British to the east, the American airborne assault did not go according to plan; but it achieved its broad objectives.

...the air picture at the airhead at Ste-Mère-Eglise gives a good impression of the difficult country into which the two US airborne divisions were dropped.

ENCLOSURES

1 Top-secret hand-drawn map showing the minute-by-minute position on the way in to the drop zone just west of Ste-Mère-Eglise for elements of the 505th Parachute Infantry Regiment of the 82nd Airborne Division.

2 Paratrooper's eye-view jump map of the drop zone at Ste-Marie-du-Mont. This town lay in the planned drop zone for the 101st Airborne Division, between Utah Beach and Carentan to the south. The map's central octagonal section is an aerial reconnaissance photograph.

RIGHT One of the "crickets" carried by US airborne troops on their D-Day jump. Used as a signalling device from the hedgerows, one click was to be answered by two...

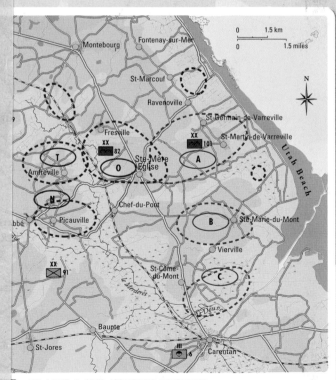

US 101ST & 82ND AIRBORNE DIVISIONS 6 JUNE 1944

- ⬭ Intended drop zone of 101st Airborne Division
- ⬭ Actual drop zone of 101st Airborne Division
- ◯ Intended drop zone of 82nd Airborne Division
- ◌ Actual drop zone of 82nd Airborne Division

UTAH BEACH

US 4TH INFANTRY DIVISION

PLANNED H-HOUR: 06.30

ALLIES

ASSAULTING DIVISION: US 4th Infantry
DIVISION COMMANDER: Major General Raymond O. Barton
INFANTRY ASSAULT UNITS: 1st and 2nd Battalions of the 8th Infantry Regiment
MEN LANDED: 23,250
CASUALTIES (DEAD, WOUNDED & MISSING): c.200

AXIS

DEFENDING DIVISIONS: Elements of 709th Infantry and 352nd Infantry
709TH INFANTRY DIVISION COMMANDER: Lieutenant General Karl-Wilhelm von Schlieben
352ND INFANTRY DIVISION COMMANDER: Lieutenant General Dietrich Kraiss

RIGHT *US Army-issue Bible carried into battle on Utah Beach in the breast pocket of Staff Sergeant Louie Havard. During D-Day an enemy bullet struck Havard's rifle, ricocheted off it and struck the Bible, which saved his life. Louie Havard survived the Second World War.*

Bad weather had already caused the postponement of the invasion by one day, and D-Day itself was launched in what Eisenhower's chief meteorologist hoped would be a brief but usable window in the weather. Conditions were very unpleasant in landing craft as they wallowed in the swell, and visibility was so poor that the bombers sent to provide last-minute softening-up of the defences at Utah and Omaha were largely ineffective.

The landings were to take place after low water on a rising tide, and local conditions meant that they would begin at 6.30 am in the US sector and 7.30 am in the British. Fast German patrol boats alerted at about 3.30 am, attacked the invasion flotilla (the only serious casualty was the Norwegian destroyer *Svenner*) and at 5.35 am, only 15 minutes before Allied warships began their own bombardment, German coastal batteries began to open fire.

Although the overriding importance of the deep water port of Cherbourg always made it desirable for a landing to take place at the base of the Cotentin, it was only when the original Cossac plan was modified early in 1944 to involve a five-division assault that planners were able to add Utah Beach to their schedule. Even then it was not ideal, for it was separated by rivers from the other beaches, and the low ground behind it had been flooded, restricting the routes inland. Major General Raymond Barton's 4th Division of VII Corps was to land there on a two-battalion front, with 36 Duplex Drive (DD) swimming tanks supporting the first wave.

There was good luck and bad. A mixture of a strong coastal current and the obscuration of navigation landmarks by the smoke of the naval

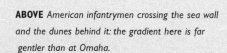

ABOVE *American infantrymen crossing the sea wall and the dunes behind it: the gradient here is far gentler than at Omaha.*

LEFT *A US soldier, carrying the light .30 M1 Carbine, moves along Utah Beach.*

bombardment meant that the whole invasion force landed about 2,000 yards further south than had been planned, and the tanks arrived late. But the area where the troops came ashore, around La Grande Dune, was actually much less heavily defended than the planned attack sector, and casualties on the run-in and the landing itself were mercifully light. There might have been confusion as junior commanders realized that they were in the wrong place, but the assistant division commander, the arthritic but dogged Brigadier General Theodore Roosevelt (son of the president of the same name) had pressed to be allowed to go ashore with the first wave. Under fire most of the day, he repeatedly led groups over the sea wall and pointed them inland. His bravery earned him the Congressional Medal of Honor, and helped ensure that within three hours of the first landing the beach was secure and cleared, with engineers and naval demolition parties dealing with beach obstacles, making gaps in the sea wall and clearing minefields. By nightfall infantry had pushed as far inland as the main Cherbourg-Bayeux road at Les Forges.

ABOVE *The watch worn on D-Day by Staff Sergeant Glen E. Gibson of the 70th Tank Battalion. Gibson was the sole survivor from the crews of four amphibious tanks which were destroyed when their landing craft hit a mine off Utah Beach. His watch was stopped by the explosion at 5.46 am.*

BELOW *American troops in foxholes on Utah while beach clearance goes on in the background.*

THEODORE ROOSEVELT Jr *was son of the president of the same name, and a brigadier general. He served in the First World War and helped create the American Legion after it. He distinguished himself as assistant division commander of 4th Infantry Division on D-Day, but died of a heart attack on 12 July, the day he was due to take command of his own division. Awarded the Congressional Medal of Honor, America's highest gallantry award, he lies buried at St-Laurent, beside his brother Quentin, killed in 1918.*

UTAH BEACH 6–8 JUNE 1944

- ■ German strongpoint
- — Front line 12.00 hrs 6 June
- — Front line 7 June
- → US advance movements
- Sandy shoreline
- Rocks
- Flooded area

POINTE DU HOC

Tuesday
6
JUNE
D-DAY

PLANNED H-HOUR: 06.30

ALLIES

ASSAULTING UNITS: D, E and F Companies of 2nd Ranger Battalion
COMMANDER: Lieutenant Colonel James E. Rudder
MEN LANDED: 225
CASUALTIES: 135 (by 8 June 1944)

AXIS

DEFENDING UNIT: Elements of 716th Coastal Defence Division
NUMBER: 200
716TH COASTAL DEFENCE DIVISION COMMANDER: Lieutenant General Wilhelm Richter

JAMES EARL RUDDER

was a college teacher and football coach with a reserve commission when he was called to active duty in 1941. He took command of 2nd Ranger Battalion in 1942, leading it in its assault on the Pointe du Hoc. Rudder was a full colonel in 1945, and subsequently combined careers as university president, civic leader and reserve officer, rising to major general. President Johnson awarded him the Distinguished Service Medal, the highest peacetime service award, in 1967.

US 2ND RANGERS BATTALION

The Pointe du Hoc (Hoe in the US Official History – the word stems from old French for a vessel's jib) was as important to the Americans as Pegasus Bridge and Merville were to the British. The clifftop site, rising 177 feet from the shore, was believed to house six 155mm guns in concrete emplacements: they could either fire onto Utah Beach or at the force assaulting Omaha. These defences had been damaged by bombing but aerial and naval bombardment could not guarantee to destroy them. Their location meant that neither parachutists nor glider troops could be used, and the mission was given to Lieutenant Colonel James E. Rudder's 2nd Ranger Battalion, which would storm from the sea.

Colonel Rudder's first wave of three companies would land at the foot of the cliffs, scale them, and then reinforced by another two companies, while his 6th company continued to Omaha, whence it would join the rest of the battalion by land. Most Rangers men would be in landing craft, but four amphibious DUKWs, fitted with turntable ladders supplied by the London Fire Brigade, mounted twin Lewis machine guns. To climb the cliffs, ropes attached to grapnels were to be fired by special projectors.

Rudder's men transferred to their landing craft and DUKWs 12 miles out, lost two craft in heavy seas, and lost two more when they ran in parallel to the coast after making the wrong landfall. Although the garrison was ready for them, the Rangers began their ascent at once, undaunted by the fact that waterlogged ropes prevented the grapnels from rising far enough. A last-minute attack by B-26 bombers rattled the defenders, and the destroyers USS *Satterlee* and HMS *Talybont* fired as the Rangers climbed. There were no guns in the casemates – they had been moved inland to escape the bombing – but Rudder's men found and destroyed them. The Rangers were then counter-attacked and forced back into the original German defences, but they held until relieved on 8 June. They lost 135 of the 225 men landed: the follow-up companies did not receive the success signal and went on to Omaha.

LEFT *US Rangers hauling ammunition up the cliff face at the Pointe du Hoc after its capture.*

BELOW *A-20s of the 9th US Air Force attacking the Pointe du Hoc (bottom right) on D-Day.*

ABOVE *The battleship USS Texas pounding the Pointe du Hoc with her 14-inch guns on D-Day. She formed part of the Western Task Force under Rear Admiral D. P. Kirk, USN.*

O.R., SEE SKETCH

585

587

588

939

TRENCHES

GUN POSITIONS DISMANTLED

4.

COVERED TRENCH

6.

5864 9381
ELEV. ABOVE
M.S.L. 115'

BLDG. REMOVED

WIRE

TOP SECRET-BIGOT
21 APRIL, 1944
PAGE 33
LAYOUT OF TYPICAL BATTERY
ILLUSTRATED BY
BATTERY 586938
POINTE DU HOE

NEPTUNE MONOGRAPH-CTF.122   TOP SECRET-BIGOT

ABOVE An Allied secret briefing map showing the German defensive positions on the Pointe du Hoc in April 1944.

LEFT This aerial reconnaissance photograph of Pointe du Hoc (the point itself is at the top of the photograph) gives a good view of the damage done by bombing before D-Day. The map overlay is a detail from the map above.

BELOW Allied bombing and naval gunfire had done terrible damage to German defences before the Rangers landed.

OMAHA BEACH

Tuesday
6
JUNE
D-DAY

PLANNED H-HOUR: 06.30

ALLIES

ASSAULTING DIVISION:
US 1st Infantry
US 1ST DIVISION COMMANDER:
Major General Clarence R. Huebner
INFANTRY ASSAULT UNITS: 2nd and
3rd Battalions of the 16th Infantry
Regiment, and 1st and 2nd Battalions of the
116th Infantry Regiment attached from US
29th Infantry Division
MEN LANDED: 34,250
CASUALTIES (DEAD, WOUNDED & MISSING): c.3,000

AXIS

DEFENDING DIVISIONS: Elements of 352nd
Infantry and 716th Coastal Defence
352ND INFANTRY DIVISION COMMANDER:
Lieutenant General Dietrich Kraiss
716TH COASTAL DEFENCE DIVISION COMMANDER:
Lieutenant General Wilhelm Richter

US 1ST INFANTRY DIVISION

Omaha was the responsibility of the US V Corps. Major General Clarence R. Huebner's 1st Division would land with two regiments abreast, the 116th Infantry (from the 29th Division) on the right and the 16th Infantry on the left. Once the beach was secured, these regiments would be supported by two other regiments, and the attackers would then seize the Bayeux road to the south and perhaps reach Isigny to the west.

The beach's gentle-sloping sand led to coarse shingle, and immediately behind rose high sandy bluffs. There were only five exits through them, and these valleys ("draws" to their attackers) were protected by concrete bunkers. Nowhere else were assaulting troops confronted with such serious obstacles. The area was defended by the over-extended 716th Division (responsible for the coastline from the Orne to the west of Omaha), but at Omaha it had been reinforced by the higher-quality 352nd Division, undetected by Allied intelligence. While the British had placed emphasis on getting specialist armoured vehicles ashore at the very beginning to deal with obstacles, the American approach was less technological, and beach-clearing was to be done by unarmoured engineer teams. Lastly, the long run-in through heavy seas caused losses before the attackers reached the shore, and the coastal current meant that most landing craft beached eastwards of their intended landfall.

At 5.40 am the first DD tanks were launched 6,000 yards out, but most foundered at once, and of the 32 only five reached the shore, doing so after the assaulting infantry. The artillery expected to fire on the way in did little better: all but one of the 105mm guns of 11th Field Artillery Battalion were lost, as were six of 7th Field Artillery Battalion's pieces. Although naval bombardment had temporarily neutralized the defences, they came to life as the landing-craft neared the shoreline, and the nine companies of the first assaulting wave were disgorged, overloaded, soaking and often sea-sick, onto the surf of a bullet-swept beach. Undamaged obstacles gave them a degree of cover but posed a terrible risk to incoming DUKWs and landing craft.

The failure of the first wave meant that the specialist engineer teams were unable to work as planned, despite suffering 40 per cent casualties that day. After the first dreadful hour the 116th Infantry had a toehold just west of Les Moulins and, as much by luck as by judgement, it was there that the regimental command group under Colonel Charles D. W. Canham and the assistant division commander, Brigadier General Norman D. Cota, landed. The view from the sea was depressing: one officer reported that beach was clogged with infantry while landing craft milled about like "a stampeded herd of cattle." Lieutenant General Omar N. Bradley, the US First Army commander, aboard USS *Augusta*, even briefly considered redirecting the remaining units to Utah Beach.

By this time there was progress on the beach as destroyers came

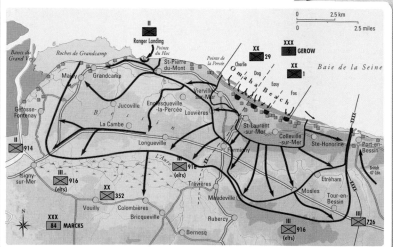

OMAHA BEACH 6–8 JUNE 1944

- ■ German strongpoint
- ◼ US positions by 12.00 hrs 6 June
- — Front line 24.00 hrs 6 June
- — Front line 7 June
- — Front line 8 June
- --- Army boundary lines
- –⋅⋅– Divisional boundary lines
- → US advance movements
- ▨ Sandy shoreline
- ▦ Rocks
- ▢ Flooded area

0   2.5 km
0   2.5 miles

BELOW *Seconds to the landing. US infantrymen in a landing craft approaching Omaha Beach. Smoke on the shoreline comes from naval gunfire supporting the landing.*

LEFT *The Purple Heart, for all US personnel wounded or killed in combat. Around 3,000 were awarded to the D-Day casualties on Omaha.*

RIGHT *The photographer Robert Capa landed at Omaha, but most of the film he shot was ruined by an over-enthusiastic developer. This photograph shows infantrymen moving through the surf and the beach defences.*

dangerously close inshore to engage defences at point-blank range, and determined groups of men fought their way off the beach. Sometimes they were formal leaders, and sometimes they were not: decorations honoured the achievements of Brigadier General Cota at one extreme and several gallant NCOs and private soldiers at the other.

By the day's end the Americans held a narrow strip of land between St-Laurent and Colleville, but they lacked most of the resources needed for the planned advance inland. Omaha Beach had cost V Corps around 3,000 casualties, more than were suffered on the other beaches in total.

ENCLOSURES

1 D-Day situation report messages sent by the US Information Team on Omaha Beach, commanded by Colonel B.B. Talley, to Major General Leonard T. Gerow ("LTG"), US V Corps Commander, who was watching developments from a ship offshore. All 21 officers and men of the Information Team were decorated for gallantry on D-Day, one of the largest single-unit awards in US Army history.

2 Terse German radio signal log times at 4.15 am on D-Day which reads, "Thouseands of ships tracked. They're coming."

3 The Wednesday 7 June 1944 edition of Stars and Stripes, the daily newspaper of the US Armed Forces in teh European Theatre of Operations, with first news of the D-Day landings. This copy was owned by Wilson Wood, who briefed Marauder bomber pilots on their D-Day missions over Utah Beach, described on the front page.

NORMAN "DUTCH" COTA was an ebullient New Englander. Assistant division commander of the 29th Division, he was the first general ashore on Omaha Beach. Showing characteristic vigour in getting men off the beach, he shouted to one group of soldiers that as Rangers, they should be leading the way. Promoted to command the 28th Division, he led it through Paris in the liberation parade, and in heavy fighting in the Hürtgen Forest. His division was badly mauled in the German Ardennes offensive.

BELOW A medic tends a wounded man on Omaha. Note the drip held by his assistant: promptly administered, intravenous saline replacements were invaluable in reducing deaths from shock.

"We **HIT** the eye of the storm. **THE BATTALION WAS DECIMATED. HELL,** after that we didn't have enough to **WHIP A CAT WITH.**"

SGT JOHN R. SLAUGHTER, D CO., 116TH INFANTRY REGIMENT, 29TH DIVISION

GOLD BEACH

Tuesday
6
JUNE
D-DAY

PLANNED H-HOUR: 07.25

ALLIES

ASSAULTING DIVISION: British 50th Division
DIVISION COMMANDER: Major General D.A.H. Graham
INFANTRY ASSAULT UNITS: 1st Battalion Hampshire Regiment, 1st Battalion Dorset Regiment, 5th Battalion East Yorkshire Regiment, 6th Battalion The Green Howards
FIRST-WAVE DD TANKS: Nottinghamshire Yeomanry, 4th/7th Royal Dragoon Guards
MEN LANDED: 24,970
CASUALTIES (DEAD, WOUNDED & MISSING): c.400

AXIS

DEFENDING DIVISIONS: Elements of 716th Coastal Defence and 352nd Infantry
716TH COASTAL DEFENCE DIVISION COMMANDER: Lieutenant General Wilhelm Richter
352ND INFANTRY DIVISION COMMANDER: Lieutenant General Dietrich Kraiss

Gold, the westernmost of the British/Canadian beaches, was to be assaulted by Major General D. A. H. Graham's 50th Division of XXX Corps, which was to advance to take Bayeux, and hook right to capture Arromanches (where the British Mulberry harbour was to be built) and then link up with the Americans. 50th Division had begun the war as a Territorial formation recruited from the north-east (its distinctive divisional flash bore TT, for Tyne-Tees), and it had fought in France in 1940 and subsequently in the Western Desert. Its regional composition had been much diluted and, sadly, dwindling numbers of British soldiers available for service in the infantry were eventually to result in its disbandment: but not before it added further lustre to its laurels on D-Day.

50th Division was to land with two brigades forward, 231st on the right and 69th on the left, with 56th Brigade following-up on the right and 151st on the left. The division had 8th Armoured Brigade under command, and this provided one regiment of DD tanks with each assaulting brigade, the Nottinghamshire Yeomanry on the right and the 4th/7th Dragoon Guards on the left. Once the beach was secure, 47th Royal Marine Commando would land and make for Port-en-Bessin on the inter-Allied boundary. In contrast to American policy, specialist armoured vehicles, of the Westminster Dragoons and 6th Assault Regiment Royal Engineers, were to land just ahead of the infantry to deal with beach obstacles, mines and the sea wall. On Gold Beach alone there were almost 2,500 obstacles of one sort or another,

BRITISH 8TH ARMOURED BRIGADE

BRITISH 50TH INFANTRY DIVISION

BELOW Infantry of a follow-up wave coming ashore from a landing craft near Ver-sur-Mer on Gold Beach.

> **❝It was a sobering sight as the HAMPSHIRES left their smaller infantry landing craft. ... MEN WERE DROPPING while still in SHALLOW WATER, to be dragged forward by their mates and left on the sand, while their comrades ran on in a purposeful steady jog trot, which betrayed NO SIGN OF PANIC.❞**
>
> TROOPER JOE MINOGUE, THE WESTMINSTER DRAGOONS

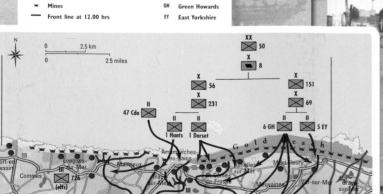

GOLD BEACH 6 JUNE 1944 UP TO 12.00 HOURS

- Area of strongest German resistance
- German resistance points
- German battery
- Mines
- Front line at 12.00 hrs

ABBREVIATIONS
Hants — Hampshire
Cdo — Commando
GH — Green Howards
EY — East Yorkshire

STAN HOLLIS was a company sergeant major in 6th Green Howards, a Yorkshire Territorial battalion, on D-Day. He personally cleared German bunkers on Mont Fleury, and later attacked a field gun in the village of Crepon. Hollis was awarded the Victoria Cross, Britain's highest award for military bravery: it was the only one given for D-Day. The citation referred to his "utmost gallantry". After the war Hollis ran a pub, and told his wife to sell his VC when he died as it was, in effect, his pension.

RIGHT Cromwell tanks of 4th County of London Yeomanry, then part of 7th Armoured Division, moving ashore from Gold Beach on 7 June.

LEFT The Victoria Cross, the highest award for gallantry awarded to British and Canadian servicemen.

BELOW British Sherman tanks move through the town of Bayeux, captured on 7 June. The first major French town to be liberated, Bayeux fell without much resistance. It was spared the terrible damage visited on Caen and St-Lô.

embodying almost 900 tons of steel, concrete or wood.

Strong defences at Le Hamel briefly held up 231st Brigade – 1st Hampshire lost its commanding officer and second-in-command – but by 8.30 the whole brigade was ashore and making progress. On the left, 69th Brigade also ran into resistance just behind the beach, but the garrisons of a battery on Mont Fleury and the village of Ver-sur-Mer had been so cowed by naval and air bombardment that they offered little opposition. With the assaulting brigades ashore, naval beachmasters began to organize the beaches so that follow-up units could land smoothly: 151st Brigade

arrived at about 11.00, with 69th Brigade not far behind. By the day's end almost 25,000 men had gone ashore.

Progress inland was encouraging. The commandos dug in overlooking Port-en-Bessin, and Arromanches was cleared by nightfall. During the advance of 69th Brigade, Company Sergeant Major Stan Hollis of the Green Howards earned the Victoria Cross, the only one awarded as a result of D-Day, for valour that began on Mont Fleury and ended in the village of Crepon. By nightfall 151st Brigade had reached the Bayeux-Caen road. Bayeux itself was hopelessly exposed, and fell the following day.

ATTACHMENT

Extract from the pocket diary of Sergeant G. E. Hughes. On D-Day, Hughes, then a corporal, landed with the 1st Battalion, Hampshire Regiment at Arromanches.

BRITISH 231ST INFANTRY BRIGADE

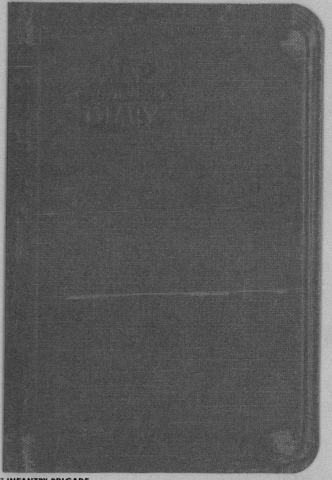

JUNO BEACH

PLANNED H-HOUR: 07.45

ALLIES

ASSAULTING DIVISION: Canadian 3rd Division
DIVISION COMMANDER: Major General R.F.L. Keller
INFANTRY ASSAULT UNITS: The Royal Winnipeg Rifles, the Regina Rifle Regiment, the Queen's Own Rifles of Canada, the North Shore (New Brunswick) Regiment
FIRST-WAVE DD TANKS: 6th Canadian Armoured Regiment, 10th Canadian Armoured Regiment
MEN LANDED: 21,500
CASUALTIES (DEAD, WOUNDED & MISSING): c.1,000

AXIS

DEFENDING DIVISION: Elements of 716th Coastal Defence Division
DIVISION COMMANDER: Lieutenant General Wilhelm Richter

Canada made a distinctive contribution to the Allied effort in both world wars, and it was fitting that Major General R. F. L. Keller's 3rd Canadian Division, part of I Corps, should land on Juno Beach. The Canadian armed forces reflected, not without tensions, Canada's cultural divide, and though most units serving overseas bore English titles and contained a majority of English-speaking officers and men, Le Régiment de Maisonneuve and Les Fusiliers Mont-Royal, for example, were to play their brave part alongside the Black Watch of Canada and the South Saskatchewan Regiment in Normandy. There were two Canadian destroyers, HMCS *Sioux* and *Algonquin*, among the warships bombarding Juno, and they reflected the Canadian navy's costly service escorting Atlantic convoys.

The attack was complicated by the fact that the coast was protected by offshore rocks, exposed at low tide, except at the mouth of the River Seulles and the small port of Courseulles, where the Germans had thickened their defences. The town was the objective of 7th Canadian Brigade, the division's right assault brigade, while 8th Canadian Brigade was to land further east, at Bernières and St-Aubin-sur-Mer. Each assaulting brigade comprised three infantry battalions and an armoured regiment. As on British beaches, specialist armour, in this case from the 22nd Dragoons and 5th and 6th Assault Regiments Royal Engineers, was to deal with the beach defences. 9th Canadian Brigade would follow 8th onto the beaches. The defenders of Juno came from thinly-spread 716th Division, which had about three companies – no more than 400 men – in the path of an attack which would put well some 2,400 men and 76 tanks ashore in its first wave.

The Canadians landed slightly later than planned, which helped them get over the offshore rocks but meant that they arrived among beach defences. The landing craft had to jockey their way in and out among obstacles and 70 out of 306 were lost or damaged. Courseulles was stubbornly defended, and did not fall until well on in the afternoon, after Royal Marine Centaur tanks

CANADIAN 3RD INFANTRY DIVISION

ABOVE *Canadian infantrymen of Le Régiment de la Chaudière, the follow-up battalion of 8th Canadian Brigade, landing near Bernières on the morning of D-Day.*

and Royal Engineer assault tanks supported the Royal Winnipeg Rifles and the Regina Rifles. Further east, the Queens Own Rifles suffered severely crossing the beach at Bernières, but soon stormed the village, and the New Brunswickers of the North Shore Regiment had a similar experience in St-Aubin. On the Canadian left, 48 (Royal Marine) Commando landing at about 9.00 am, lost landing craft to the now-submerged beach obstacles, and was galled by machine gun fire from St-Aubin, but swung left to capture Lagrune-sur-Mer, on the boundary with the British 3rd Division. Although the Canadians ended the day in contact with 50th Division on their right, and just short of the Bayeux-Caen road to their front, there remained a gap between them and Sword Beach on their left.

BELOW *Men of 48 (Royal Marine) Commando going ashore on Nan, the easternmost sector of Juno Beach.*

JUNO BEACH 6 JUNE 1944 UP TO 12.00 HOURS

		ABBREVIATIONS	
▪	Area of strongest German resistance	RWR	Royal Winnipeg
●	German resistance points	RR	Regina Rifles
♔	German battery	QOR	Queens Own Rifles
⊷	Mines	NSR	North Shore Regiment
—	Front line at 12.00 hrs	RM Cdo	Royal Marine Commando

ACTIVE SERVICE

A.E. W307B.

C & Co (b) Ltd

[Crown Copyright]

This envelope must not be used for coin or valuables. It cannot be accepted for registration.

NOTE:—

Correspondence in this envelope need not be censored Regimentally. The contents are liable to examination at the Base.

The following Certificate must be signed by the writer:—

I certify on my honour that the contents of this envelope refer to nothing but private and family matters.

Signature
Name only

[Up to three letters may be forwarded in this Cover, but these must be all from same writer. The cover should be address in such case to the Base Censor.]

Address :—

D-DAY REX64 33.07B

HOBART'S "FUNNIES"

Major General Sir Percy Hobart, brother-in-law of General Montgomery, was recalled from retirement in 1941, at the instigation of Winston Churchill, to take command of the 79th Armoured Division and mastermind the development of specially adapted armour to support a seaborne invasion. The "funnies", as they were known, were invaluable on Sword, Gold and Juno for facilitating rapid exit of the first waves of infantry and support vehicles off the beaches.

BELOW A standard M4 Sherman tank with a revolving drum fitted to a frontally extended frame, known as a "flail tank" or "crab". The chains attached to the drum exploded mines and cleared belts of barbed wire, leaving a safe path for following troops.

ABOVE A Duplex Drive (DD) Sherman tank with a collapsible canvas screen, which, when raised, gave it sufficient buoyancy to float. It had two propellers and a top speed in the water of over 4 knots. Amphibious armour was used for the first time on D-Day and gave the first-wave infantry invaluable fire support which came as a complete surprise to the German defenders.

ENCLOSURE

Letter from Canadian Lance Sergeant Edwin Owen Worden to his wife, written on the boat while waiting to cross the Channel on 5 June. Worden served with the 1st Battalion, Regina Rifle Regiment. He survived D-Day but died in Holland during the Allied advance in April 1945.

ABOVE Anti-tank obstacles in the streets of St-Aubin-sur-Mer. The soldier taking cover from snipers is probably a member of the North Shore (New Brunswick) Regiment.

RIGHT Sherman tanks of 3rd Canadian Armoured Brigade using an artificial trackway built by engineers to move up the beach: a sharp contrast to Dieppe (see page 6).

SWORD BEACH

PLANNED H-HOUR: 07.25

ALLIES

ASSAULTING DIVISION: British 3rd Division

DIVISION COMMANDER: Major General T. G. Rennie

INFANTRY ASSAULT UNITS: 1st South Lancashire Regiment, 2nd East Yorkshire Regiment

FIRST-WAVE DD TANKS: 13th/18th Hussars

MEN LANDED: 28,845

CASUALTIES (DEAD, WOUNDED & MISSING): c.630

AXIS

DEFENDING DIVISION: Elements of 716th Coastal Defence Division

DIVISION COMMANDER: Lieutenant General Wilhelm Richter

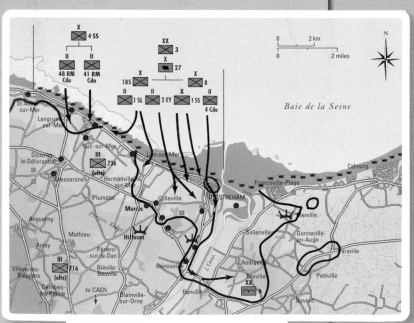

SWORD BEACH 6 JUNE 1944 UP TO 12.00 HOURS

▦ Area of strongest German resistance	**ABBREVIATIONS**
● German resistance points	SS Special Service
♛ German battery	RM Cdo Royal Marine Commando
⌐ Mines	SL South Lancashire
▬ Front line at 12.00 hrs	EY East Yorkshire

Sword, the easternmost invasion beach, was the objective of Major General T. G. Rennie's 3rd Division. This division had fought (under Montgomery's command) in 1940, but had not been engaged since. Its task was important and complex. Inland was the city of Caen, capital of Normandy and an important communication hub. Montgomery believed that its early capture was crucial because it would give him room for manoeuvre on the British flank. 3rd Division's orders specified that by nightfall it was to have "captured or effectively masked" the city. Next, the division had to facilitate a link with 6th Airborne Division via Pegasus Bridge, though the commandos of 1st Special Service Brigade, landing on the eastern edge of Sword Beach and taking Ouistreham, were going to make the junction. Finally, it was known that the only German armour close enough to launch a counter-attack, 21st Panzer Division, was in the area, so it was likely that 3rd Division would encounter German armour.

The presence of offshore rocks and the proximity of the mouth of the Orne and the town of Ouistreham meant that 3rd Division landed on the front of a single brigade, which made its deployment sequential rather than simultaneous. The leading brigade, 8th, used two of its battalions, 1st South Lancashire and 2nd East Yorkshire, to secure the coastal strip, and then pushed its third battalion, 1st Suffolk, assisted by tanks of the 13th/18th Hussars, inland to attack a German battery near Colleville and a strongpoint codenamed Hillman just south of the same village. This took longer than had been expected, largely because Hillman, which had not been bombed or shelled, was too serious an obstacle for the Suffolks to take, save by a formal attack with proper armoured support. As long as Hillman remained in German hands it acted like a cork in the bottle.

The next brigade to land, 185th, had been ordered to capture Caen, with the infantry of 2nd King's Shropshire Light Infantry riding on tanks of the Staffordshire Yeomanry to spearhead the advance. However, the narrowness of the front and congestion on and behind the beach caused delay, and although the leading elements of the brigade eventually reached the northern edge of Lebisey Wood, just

BRITISH 3RD INFANTRY DIVISION

LORD LOVAT or Shimi to his friends, came from a Highland family with a stormy past – an ancestor was the last peer beheaded for treason. He joined the Commandos in 1940, and led 4 Commando on the Dieppe raid, capturing a coastal battery. On D-Day he was accompanied ashore on Sword Beach by his piper, Bill Millin, and carried a hunting rifle. He was later severely wounded, and after the war acted as Churchill's emissary to Stalin before becoming a noted cattle breeder.

BELOW Commandos of Brigadier Lord Lovat's 1st Special Service Brigade, destined to relieve the paratroops at Pegasus Bridge, landing at La Brèche in the Queen Red sector.

❝I started the pipes up and marched UP and DOWN. This sergeant came running over, 'GET DOWN YOU MAD BASTARD. YOU'RE ATTRACTING ATTENTION ON US.' ANYWAY I CONTINUED marching up and down until we moved off the beach.❞

PIPER BILL MILLIN, 1ST SPECIAL SERVICE BRIGADE

Sapper Fred Sadler

Sapper Cyril Hawkins

Sapper Jimmy Leask

PHILIPPE KIEFFER

was born in Haiti to a family originating in Alsace. A reserve officer aboard the old battleship Courbet in 1940, he immediately joined the Free French forces. Impressed by British commandos, he raised the first French commando unit. He led 177 of his men ashore on Sword Beach, and took the casino in Ouistreham and the lock gates on the canal: his commandos suffered heavy casualties and he was twice wounded. After the war he sat in the National Assembly.

three miles short of Caen, they were unable to get further. When 9th Brigade arrived, after further delay, Major General Rennie ordered it to defend the Orne bridges against attack from the west. His concern was understandable, for he had already heard that 21st Panzer Division had begun its counter-attack.

21st Panzer had been re-raised to replace the original division, lost in North Africa. Its commander lacked relevant experience: on the dawn of the invasion it was inconveniently close to the Orne and the Caen Canal, and it took time for a decision to attack west of the water obstacles. Colonel von Oppeln-Bronikowski's battle group was launched northwards, but was sharply engaged by tanks and anti-tank guns, well posted on the Perières ridge, west

ABOVE *The scene on Queen White sector of Sword Beach at about 8.30 am on D-Day. Sappers of 84 Field Company Royal Engineers are in the foreground. In the background are men of 1st Battalion the Suffolk Regiment and Lord Lovat's commandos.*

of Hillman, and though it just reached the coast between the 3rd British Division and the 3rd Canadian Division, it achieved little. Although 3rd Division had shrugged off the only major D-Day counter-attack, it had failed to take Caen. With the benefit of hindsight it seems that the plan was too ambitious given the proximity of German armour and the need to squeeze all attacking brigades, one by one, across the same beach.

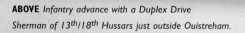

ABOVE *Infantry advance with a Duplex Drive Sherman of 13th/18th Hussars just outside Ouistreham.*

VILLERS-BOCAGE

Monday
12
JUNE
D+6

Thursday
15
JUNE
D+9

RIGHT *German tanks, heavily camouflaged and well spaced out to minimize the risk of air attack, moving up near Villers-Bocage.*

7TH ARMOURED DIVISION *originated as the Mobile Division, formed in Egypt in 1938, and fought throughout the desert campaign, moving on to Italy before being recalled for the invasion of Europe. The division, with its extensive experience in the Mediterranean, and a measure of war-weariness, initially found the new conditions of Normandy trying, and its commander, Major General G. W. E. J. Erskine (above) was replaced. However, the division rose above the summer's misfortunes, and it took the surrender of Hamburg and participated in the 1945 Berlin victory parade. Its Gerboa badge and nickname "Desert Rats" have been inherited by the modern 7th Armoured Brigade.*

Despite bloody Omaha and British failure to take Caen, D-Day was a triumph: by its close over 130,000 Allied soldiers had been landed. Over the next few days the Allies consolidated their position. First contact between British and Americans was made on 7 June, and on the 9th American troops from Utah and Omaha met. The Allies now had a continuous beachhead, although it took more fighting to secure the Carentan area and make the link between the two US corps really secure.

Having failed to take Caen early, Montgomery ordered XXX Corps to attack through Villers-Bocage and Noyers, cross the River Odon, and then push south and south-east of Tilly-sur-Seulles, outflanking Caen. Major General G. W. E. J. Erskine's 7th Armoured Division was to lead, with 22nd Armoured Brigade at its head. On 10 June the advance began, but the bocage of little fields bounded by thick hedges was easier to defend than attack. Infantry from 56th Infantry Brigade, borrowed from 50th Division, came up that night, and the advance was resumed with infantry on hand to help with close-quarter fighting, but progress was again poor.

On 12 June 7th Armoured tried again, this time with its own infantry of 131st Brigade to help. It had crossed the River Aure and swung south so that at nightfall on the 11th its leading elements were only two miles from Caumont and five from Villers-Bocage, which was taken without difficulty on the 12th. But as the leading elements of 4th County of London Yeomanry with infantry of the Rifle Brigade moved out along the Caen road, they were assailed by a tank company commanded by SS Captain Michael Wittmann; he knocked out 12 tanks, 13 troop carriers and two anti-tank guns. Although his own tank was destroyed, he and his crew escaped. As the counter-attack gained momentum, Major General Erskine decided, with his corps commander's approval, to pull back to Tracy-Bocage, and then fell back on Livery. The action, termed "disappointing" by the British official history, was eventually to contribute to both divisional and corps commanders losing their jobs.

ABOVE *German tanks moving up the battle area were repeatedly harried from the air. This photograph of Lancaster heavy bombers in action shows what the original caption calls a "really good concentration of bomb bursts" on German armour at Villers-Bocage.*

> **"[THE TIGER]** immediately knocked out COLONEL **ARTHUR'S** tank, and that of the regimental second in command, **MAJOR CARR**, whom he seriously wounded, followed by the Regimental Sergeant Major's tank. Captain Dyas in the **FOURTH TANK**, reversed and backed into the front garden of a **NEARBY HOUSE."**
>
> MAJOR W. H. J. SALE, 4TH COUNTY OF LONDON YEOMANRY

ABOVE
A knocked-out Cromwell tank of 4th County of London Yeomanry in the main street of Villers-Bocage.

MICHAEL WITTMANN was

one of the war's most outstanding tank commanders. Between March 1943 and January 1944 his Tiger of 1st SS Panzer Division destroyed over a hundred Russian tanks and assault guns. Transferred to Normandy in command of an SS heavy tank company, he distinguished himself at Villers-Bocage, adding swords and oak leaves to his Knight's Cross. On 8 August, during Operation Totalize, his tank was knocked out by a Sherman of the 1st Northamptonshire Yeomanry with no survivors.

BELOW The Tiger tank with its 88mm gun. Although slower than the Sherman, and less mechanically reliable, its thick armour and fearsome fire power made it a formidable defensive weapon in Normandy. The Allies reckoned that on average it cost them three tanks to knock out one Tiger.

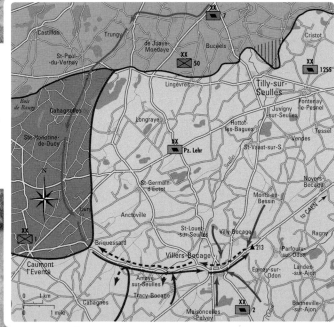

VILLERS-BOCAGE 11–13 JUNE 1944

— Front line 24.00 hrs 11 June
— Front line 24.00 hrs 24 June
↗ Advance of 7th Armoured Division 12 June to 24.00 hrs
↗ Advance of 7th Armoured Division 13 June
↗ German counter-attacks 13 June
↙ Retreat of 7th Armoured Division 13 June
↗ German counter-attacks 14 June
↙ Retreat of 7th Armoured Division 14 June
▓ British withdraw from salient 12 June

PLUTO & MULBERRY

MULBERRIES IN USE:
12 JUNE–
28 NOVEMBER 1944

PERSONNEL LANDED:	231,315
VEHICLES LANDED:	45,181
TONS OF STORES LANDED:	628,000

The Allies had a huge logistic appetite: indeed, from 15 to 19 June they landed a daily average of almost 35,000 men, 25,000 tons of stores, and 5,894 vehicles. It was evident that the Germans would fight hard to retain Cherbourg, the only major port in the area. When its commander surrendered on 26 June, the docks had already been smashed. But a shortfall in port capacity had long been identified, and in 1941 a War Office port engineering branch was formed under Major (later Brigadier Sir Bruce) White. The Admiralty contributed through the Department of Miscellaneous Weapons Development and the Department of Naval Constructors, and US engineers also became involved. Both Churchill and Admiral Lord Louis Mountbatten, first director of Combined Operations, acted as the project's "godfathers". Dieppe lent urgency, by suggesting that the Allies would not capture a port intact.

In September 1943 instructions were issued for the construction of two harbours, Mulberry A for the Americans and Mulberry B for the British. They were to be made in Britain, towed across the Channel, and were to handle 12,000 tons of stores a day, about one-third of the total requirement. Concrete caissons (Phoenix) formed the harbour wall. They would be sheltered by breakwaters (Gooseberries) consisting of blockships and floating bombardons (Corncobs) and connected to the shore by floating roadways (Whales). The first blockships, old vessels sailing under their own steam, were sunk on 7 June. One of the stores piers of Mulberry B took loads from coasters into trucks on 14 June, and the first tank landed at Mulberry A two days later.

On 18 June the weather turned very ugly, and did not improve till the 22nd. Mulberry A was crippled and Mulberry B damaged, but was soon brought back into service. The Americans succeeded in landing stores over open beaches or into small ports, and although the piers and roadway of Mulberry A had disappeared the Gooseberries still proved invaluable. By the end of October about 25 per cent of stores, 20 per cent of personnel and 15 per cent of vehicles had been landed through Mulberry. The development of the DUKW, essentially an amphibious truck, probably made the floating roadways redundant, but this would not have been obvious in 1943.

As early as November 1939 it had been suggested that petrol could be supplied to the continent by undersea pipe, and Pluto (Pipeline Under the Ocean) was the child of discussions between the Chief of Combined Operations and the Petroleum Warfare Department in 1942. Two pipes ran from Sandown, Isle of Wight, to terminals (one British and one American) near Port-en-Bessin, and another later ran from Dungeness to a terminal near Boulogne. The Normandy Pluto did not become operational till the end of July; until then the Allies received fuel via Tombola, buoyed pipelines connected to tankers moored offshore, which in theory (but seldom in practice) delivered 8,000 tons a day.

BELOW *One of the gigantic spools, codenamed Conundrums, which unrolled Pluto, the cross-Channel pipeline.*

ABOVE *A shore terminal for Tombola, which enabled tankers to pipe fuel ashore. Many of the US troops of the Petroleum Distribution Group had been oil workers in civilian life.*

LEFT The floating roadway of the British Mulberry at Arromanches, photographed on 14 June, its third day of operation.

RIGHT Storm damage sustained by one of the piers at Mulberry A. The American harbour was ruined by the storm, and supply briefly faltered.

LEFT Churchill visited Normandy soon after D-Day. This photograph shows his evident satisfaction in an invention he had done so much to support.

BELOW Mulberry B at work. An outer line of caissons provided shelter from the waves and enabled some vessels to be unloaded into DUKWs, while vehicles could be landed on the floating pierheads and driven ashore along the piers.

OPERATION EPSOM

Saturday
24
JUNE
D+18

Friday
30
JUNE
D+24

BRITISH 49TH INFANTRY DIVISION

The great storm came at a bad moment for the Allies, for both were preparing offensives: the Americans into the Cotentin, heading for Cherbourg, and further south, towards St-Lô, while the British were gearing up for another attempt to take Caen. Despite the damage sustained by the Mulberries, the Gooseberries, which had been inserted off the other invasion beaches, did rather better, though that at Utah was damaged. However, the storm reduced the pace of Allied build-up, and enabled the Germans to shift extra forces into Normandy to buttress their front.

The next British attack was to consist of a minor attack east of the Orne, in which 152nd Brigade of 51st Highland Division was to

LEFT *Royal Scots Fusiliers walk forward into the mist on the first day of Epsom.*

BELOW *Infantrymen of 6th Royal Scots Fusiliers, part of the 15th (Scottish) Division, on 26 June 1944, ready to advance under a lowering sky.*

capture the village of Ste-Honorine-de-la-Chardonnerette, just south of 6th Airborne Division's old dropping zones. The storm delayed the attack until 23 June but it proved successful, and the village was secured by midday. An altogether larger venture was Operation Epsom, on the other side of Caen, which was to involve part of both the bruised XXX Corps and the newly-arrived but still incomplete VIII Corps under Lieutenant General Sir Richard O'Connor. There were over 700 guns available to support the attack, and three cruisers and the monitor HMS *Roberts* were also to assist. The main blow was to fall between Tilly-sur-Seulles in the west and Carpiquet, not far from Caen, in the east.

On 25 June 49th Division of XXX Corps, fighting its first battle, attacked Juvigny, Vendes and Rauray in an effort to secure the eastern shoulder of the attack sector, and though it made some progress it failed to take the Rauray spur, which caused repeated trouble over the next few days. The following morning, in weather so bad that flying was out of the question and cross-country going poor, VIII Corps struck out for the Odon but did not quite reach it,

RICHARD O'CONNOR *was commissioned into the Cameronians in 1909 and was a temporary lieutenant colonel in 1918. He made his reputation commanding the British attack into the Western Desert in December 1941, but was unluckily captured soon afterwards. Escaping from captivity after the Italian surrender in 1943, he was a corps commander in Normandy, but never really regained his old touch for armoured warfare. Adjutant general of the army after the war, he resigned on a point of principle in 1947.*

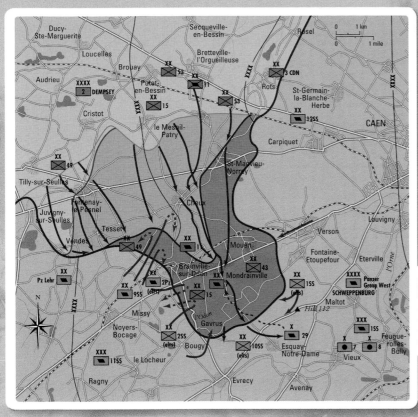

OPERATION EPSOM
24–30 JUNE 1944

Front line 24 June
Front line 25 June
Front line 26 June
Front line 30 June

ABOVE Infantrymen, on the lookout for snipers, approach a breached wall in the village of St-Manvieu on the left of 15th (Scottish) Division's attack.

PAUL HAUSSER

had a conventional army career, retiring as a major general in 1932, but joining the SS two years later. Badly wounded as a divisional commander on the Eastern Front, in June 1944 he commanded 2nd SS Panzer Corps, and counter-attacked Operation Epsom. However, his plan fell into Allied hands and the attack failed. He took command of 7th Army on 29 June. Hausser escaped from the Falaise pocket and, an SS colonel general, commanded an army group until dismissed in 1945.

though a bridge was seized intact the next day by 15th (Scottish) Division. The Scots were supported by the tanks of 11th Armoured Division and 31st Tank Brigade, in a bitter battle with attacks meeting stern resistance and repeated counter-attacks. By nightfall on the 28th there was a salient five miles deep but only two wide into the German lines, and it had attracted most of the German armoured reserves. A series of counter-attacks, which peaked on 1 July, were beaten off, and the battle ended with the British secure across the Odon south-west of Caen, but still without sufficient leverage to wrest that city from the Germans. In one sense Epsom had failed, and had cost 15th Division alone 2,500 casualties. But it had blunted the cutting edge of German armour so badly that there was no longer any chance of it mounting a comprehensive counter-attack on the Allied bridgehead.

BRITISH 11TH ARMOURED DIVISION

15TH SCOTTISH INFANTRY DIVISION

ABOVE The advance goes on, with a Churchill tank of 31st Tank Brigade moving up in support.

LEFT Firefight in a hedgeline: men of 6th Royal Scots Fusiliers, with a Bren light machine gun in the centre of the picture.

BOCAGE FIGHTING & CHERBOURG

Tuesday
6
JUNE
D-DAY

Tuesday
27
JUNE
D+21

JOE COLLINS

was commissioned into the infantry in 1917, and was commanding a division in Hawaii when war broke out in 1941. His tough style gained him the nickname "Lightning Joe", and he was selected to command VII Corps in the invasion of Europe. In 1944 he came to notice as conqueror of Cherbourg, and was photographed with his defeated opponent Lieutenant General Karl-Wilhelm von Schlieben, commander of 709th Infantry Division and the Cherbourg garrison (pictured above left).

The terrain of Normandy presented sharp contrasts. The area around Caen and Falaise was open, with big fields whose wheat stood almost shoulder high. Further west the ground grew more enclosed. The Bessin, around Bayeux, was noted for lush pastures and apple orchards: apples and cream still define cooking *à la Normande*. John Ruskin declared in 1848 that the Cotentin resembled Worcestershire but was even more beautiful. To its south, around St-Lô, came Norman bocage in its most extreme form, a chequerboard of little fields, stout hedges on high banks, and sunken lanes which reminded visitors of Devon or Dorset.

The advance on Cherbourg through the Cotentin was comparatively straightforward, and Lieutenant General "Lighting Joe" Collins of the US VII Corps defined it, just after the great storm, as "the major effort of the American army." The attack began in earnest on 22 June, with 9th and 79th Divisions moving against the city after heavy air attack, while 4th Division sealed it off from the east. The Germans fought well, their commander, Lieutenant General Karl-Wilhelm von Schlieben, enjoined by Hitler to "defend the last bunker and leave to the enemy not a harbour but a field of ruins." Three days later Schlieben told Rommel that the city's fall was inevitable and "further sacrifices cannot alter

anything," but was again ordered to "fight to the last cartridge. ..." The powerful Fort du Roule fell that day, and Schlieben himself was captured on the 26th, though he refused to surrender his command, and sporadic fighting flickered on a little longer.

US 79TH INFANTRY DIVISION

Although Hitler ordered Rundstedt to consider a large armoured counter-attack, the opening of Operation Epsom drew German reserves to the east, and Hitler concluded that, for the moment, he would have to fight "a war of attrition" to confine the Allies to their beachhead. This was significantly smaller than planners had hoped, leading to problems in getting the right balance of combat and support troops into the lodgement area, and reducing the programme of airfield construction, notably on the open country around Caen.

Bradley's First US Army began its thrust south at the beginning of July. Reports that the fall of Cherbourg had led to a sharp diminution in German fighting power soon proved incorrect as the advance ran into determined defenders strongly

US 9TH INFANTRY DIVISION

An American infantryman dashes across a street whose German sign proclaims it the Cherbourg West Diversion.

Umgehungsstrasse Cherbourg-West

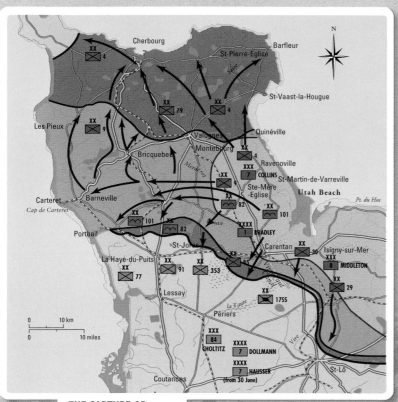

THE CAPTURE OF CHERBOURG 13–30 JUNE 1944

— Front line 13 June
— Front line 19 June
— Front line 30 June

ABOVE

Coder-decoder machine used by US troops in the field to send and receive coded messages.

posted in difficult country. US casualties were heavy: 325th Glider Infantry Regiment of 82nd Airborne, with an establishment of 135 officers and 2,838 men, had 55 officers and 1,245 men on 2 July but 41 officers and 956 men four days later: its strongest rifle company had 57 men, its weakest just 12. Junior leadership was at a premium: in 359th Infantry one company and two leaderless platoons of another were commanded by Private Barney H. Prosser. It was clear that there would be no easy ride through the bocage.

ABOVE *Although billed as a combat shot of the advance on Cherbourg, the photograph's careful composition suggests a measure of posing.*

BELOW *Major General Collins talking to an American captain at Fort du Roule, one of the last German defences to fall before the capture of Cherbourg.*

Happy warriors? Defenders of Cherbourg march past a statue of Napoleon on their way to prisoner of war cages. The censor has obliterated background detail which would have revealed how badly damaged the docks were.

43

OPERATION CHARNWOOD

Friday **7** JULY D+31

Sunday **9** JULY D+33

BRITISH 59TH INFANTRY DIVISION

At the beginning of July Caen still denied Montgomery room for manoeuvre on the eastern flank of the battlefield. The Canadians captured Carpiquet and its airfield from their old enemies, 12th SS Panzer Division, on 4 July, and on the night of the 7th 450 Lancasters and Halifaxes of RAF Bomber Command, used for the first time in direct support of ground forces, struck Caen itself. The city had already been badly damaged by bombing and by shelling from land and sea – a shell from HMS *Rodney* had felled the fine Gothic spire of the church of St-Pierre – and the preparations for the final Allied assault put the last dreadful touches to its martyrdom. One of the British soldiers who entered the city on 9 July thought it "just a waste of brick and stone, like a field of corn that has been ploughed."

The attack on Caen was carried out by I Corps. While 59th and 3rd Divisions attacked from the north, 3rd Canadian Division struck south-eastwards. The British official history acknowledges that, while the Germans used snipers and mortars to contest the advance through the city, "these gave little trouble compared with the bomb craters, the rubble and the large blocks of locally quarried stone which choked the narrow streets." The attacking corps lost about 3,500 men, and of its opponents, the infantry of 12th SS Panzer Division was reduced to battalion strength and 16th Luftwaffe Field Division had lost three-quarters of its men.

With Caen at last secured, the British mounted a limited operation to widen the bridgehead over the Odon created by Operation Epsom. 43rd Wessex Division, supported by two tank brigades and a Highland infantry brigade and abundant artillery, struck out at Hill 112 in an attack that produced "a battle of shattering intensity even by the standards of Normandy" and cost the British 2,000 casualties. By its end the men from those county regiments, which rarely caught the headlines but always formed the solid weight of the British army, held half the hill, and its long, low crest now bears their memorial.

BELOW RIGHT *Repeated bombing did terrible damage to the ancient city of Caen. This RAF photograph was taken in the first week of the Normandy campaign.*

BELOW *A Bren-gunner and riflemen in the ruins, amongst blocks of the locally-quarried pierre de Caen.*

"The TOMMY ATTACKS with GREAT MASSES OF INFANTRY and MANY TANKS. We fight AS LONG AS POSSIBLE, but by the time the survivors try to pull back, we realize that we ARE SURROUNDED."

PRIVATE ZIMMER, 12TH SS PANZER DIVISION

ENCLOSURES

1 First-aid instruction leaflet issued to British troops in Normandy to help them deal with battle casualties before the arrival of trained medics.

2 Two propaganda leaflets dropped on Allied troops in Normandy by the Luftwaffe. Although the Allies had almost total air superiority by day, in the early days of the Normandy campaign the Luftwaffe had more freedom of action during the hours of darkness.

ABOVE A section of Royal Engineers moving into Caen to deal with booby traps and unexploded bombs.

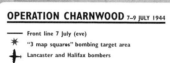

OPERATION CHARNWOOD 7–9 JULY 1944

— Front line 7 July (eve)

✳ "3 map squares" bombing target area

✚ Lancaster and Halifax bombers

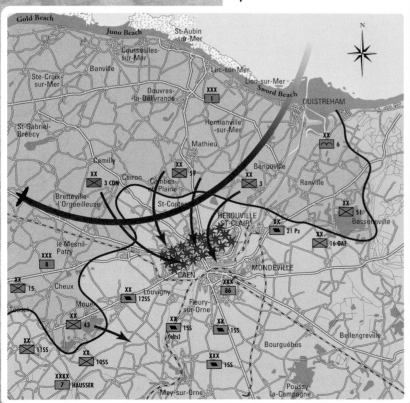

ABOVE A British sniper in Caen. Despite his camouflaged helmet and firing position, he is running a risk by being so close to the open window.

RIGHT A British soldier gives a helping hand to an old lady amid the utter desolation of Caen. One soldier wrote of the inhabitants that "one could hardly look them in the face, knowing who had done this."

BATTLE FOR ST-LO

Monday
3
JULY
D+27

Wednesday
19
JULY
D+43

OMAR BRADLEY

graduated from West
Point in 1915 but saw no
overseas service in the
First World War. In 1941

he jumped from lieutenant colonel to brigadier general,
and commanded divisions before taking over II Corps. In
Sicily his corps was under Patton's US Seventh Army, but
when Bradley commanded US ground troops in
Normandy, Patton was under his command.
A competent, level-headed general, Bradley tolerated
Montgomery better than many. He was later US Army
Chief of Staff and chairman of the Joint Chiefs.

RIGHT *The perils of the*
bocage: an American patrol
under air-burst artillery fire.

The Germans had restructured their chain of command. Field Marshal Günther von Kluge replaced Rundstedt (retired for the penultimate time) as Commander in Chief West, and on 17 July also took over Army Group B when Rommel was wounded by strafing RAF aircraft. Panzer Group West (General Heinrich Eberbach) was responsible for the British sector, and 7th Army, commanded by SS General Paul Hausser (who had replaced Colonel General Friedrich Dollmann) was facing the Americans. Hausser had two corps, LXXXIV towards the coast and II Parachute inland. Although many of the latter's men were parachutists in name only, their robust morale, numerous automatic weapons and plentiful anti-tank *Panzerfaust* made them ideal for this sort of fighting.

The chief objective of Lieutenant General Omar Bradley's First US Army

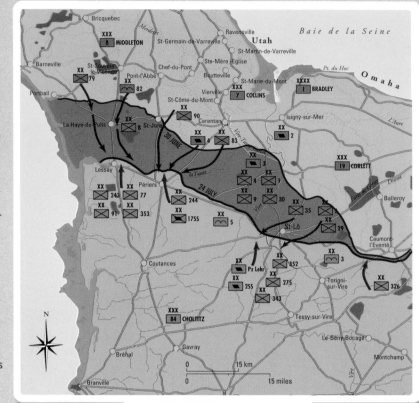

BATTLE FOR ST-LO 30 JUNE–24 JULY 1944

—— Front line 30 June	▨ Sandy shoreline
▬▬ Front line 24 July	▦ Rocks
➔ US advance movements	░ Flooded area

was the town of St-Lô, as important, in its way, to western Normandy as Caen was to the east, and which, like Caen, had been heavily bombed. It was an important traffic centre, but had, as the US official history admits, accrued psychological value so that its retention or capture "would have a strong effect on the morale of the opposing forces." It lay in the sector attacked by XIX Corps, commanded by Major General Charles H. Corlett. The key to St-Lô was the long Martinville Ridge, crowned by

US 29TH INFANTRY DIVISION

Point 192, east of the city. The central part of the ridge was attacked by 29th Division of XIX Corps, while Point 192 was assailed by 2nd Division of Major General Leonard T. Gerow's V Corps.

Point 192 fell on 11 July after being hit by 45 tons of shells, and its capture enabled the Americans to look along the ridge towards XIX Corps' objective. After slow progress by 29th Division on 11–12 July, Corlett committed his reserve, the 35th Division, and on 16 July, after a bitter see-saw battle, it took Point 122, the highest point of the ridge in the corps sector. 29th Division entered St-Lô on 18 July, taking with it the flag-draped coffin of Major Thomas D. Howie, commander of 3rd Battalion 116th Infantry, whose last radio message had announced characteristically: "Will do."

ABOVE *An American tank destroyer (a self-propelled anti-tank gun with a limited turret traverse and open top) dealing, at close range, with German positions in St-Lô.*

RIGHT *An American convoy entering St-Lô, a town terribly scarred by Allied bombing.*

OPERATION GOODWOOD

Tuesday **18** JULY **D+42**

Friday **21** JULY **D+45**

ABOVE *The British Cromwell tank was armed with one 75mm gun and two 7.9mm Besa machine guns, but was outclassed by the German Panther.*

Montgomery was still overall ground force commander, although his days as such were numbered: the Americans would form an army group once they had sufficient troops, leaving Montgomery commanding the Anglo-Canadian 21st Army Group while Bradley stepped up to command the US 12th Army Group. On 10 July Montgomery outlined his plan for the break-out. The Americans were to burst out of the bocage, exploiting down to Brittany and round to Le Mans and Alençon. But before this the British would mount their own offensive, Operation Goodwood. The timings for both operations slipped: it took the Americans longer than expected to secure St-Lô, and bad weather delayed Goodwood.

We cannot be certain whether Goodwood was intended to attract German armour, or was in fact a genuine attempt at a breakout. Major General "Pip" Roberts, of 11th Armoured Division, thought that Falaise was his objective, and Lieutenant General Miles Dempsey, of 2nd Army, believed it was "more than possible that the Huns will break" enabling him to exploit. Even Montgomery told the Chief of the Imperial General Staff that he hoped to "loose a corps of three armoured divisions into the open country about the Caen-Falaise road." Montgomery was subject to increasing pressure to expand the beachhead, and in particular to seize more ground for the construction of airfields. Moreover, he proposed to use heavy bombers to prepare the way for Goodwood, and knew that he would not get them save for an operation of first importance.

The plan was simple enough. Three armoured divisions, the Guards, 7th and 11th, would attack through a narrow corridor between the Orne and the Bois de Bavent, fanning out as soon as there was space, to take the Bourgebus Ridge and exploit beyond it. On the morning of 18 July more than 2,000 RAF and US bombers

THE GUARDS ARMOURED DIVISION

OPERATION GOODWOOD 18–21 JULY 1944

➤ British and Canadian advance 18 July
- ➤ British armoured divisions' advance 18 July
— Front line dawn 18 July
— Front line 24.00 hrs 18 July
— Front line dawn 21 July

FAR RIGHT *The impact of strategic bombers, 18 July. Some bombs were fused to explode instantaneously, leaving only small craters which would not impede the advance.*

MILES DEMPSEY *was an infantry officer in the First World War. He did well as a brigadier in 1940, and Montgomery requested him as a corps commander after El Alamein. Thereafter Dempsey moved in Montgomery's wake, commanding 2nd Army from early 1944. He was easy to work with, and Bradley applauded his lack of "jealousy or anger". He made little mark as a commander, probably because he saw himself as Montgomery's loyal lieutenant. Goodwood was essentially his plan though, and he was optimistic that it would achieve a breakthrough.*

attacked the little villages forming a framework of defence, and 11th Armoured Division moved off on the heels of the bombing. So narrow was its corridor that it led with a single regiment – 3rd Royal Tanks – and it was not until the advance was well under way that another regiment, 2nd Fife and Forfar Yeomanry, could come up. The first line of defence, furnished by the unlucky 16th Luftwaffe Field Division, was shattered by the bombing, and serious damage had also been done to 21st Panzer Division behind it. But the defence gradually came to life. Tough-minded officers like Major Hans von Luck, who ordered an anti-aircraft battery commander, at pistol point, to take on advancing tanks, animated the defence, and SS General Sepp Dietrich, commanding 1st SS Panzer Corps, ordered up reinforcements.

The 3rd Royal Tanks were beginning to climb the ridge when they were engaged by 88mm anti-tank guns, and Sherman after Sherman burst into flames. Although the British eventually secured the villages atop the ridge, any chance of a breakthrough had gone. When the battle ended on 20 July, 2nd Army had lost over 400 tanks and 6,000 men. If the tanks could be replaced from stocks in the beachhead, the loss of manpower was more serious, for this was an army scraping the bottom of its recruiting barrel. Montgomery admitted that he was over-optimistic at a press conference on the 18th, and Eisenhower was "as blue as indigo" about poor progress. Much had gone wrong in Goodwood. But one fact was undeniable: it had indeed attracted German armour to the east.

"There was a **POOR LAD** who had had most of the bottom of his back **BLOWN AWAY**. ... That poor devil screamed for about two hours; **MORPHINE** seemed to have no effect. ... Our sergeant had been in the war **FROM THE START**, and even he was white and **SHAKEN**."

PRIVATE ROBERT BOLTON, THE QUEEN'S ROYAL REGIMENT

ABOVE *British tanks moving up for Operation Goodwood. Marshalling the three attacking armoured divisions, each with more than 3,000 vehicles, including almost 300 tanks, was no easy task.*

BELOW *A Sherman passes a knocked-out German tank near the village of Cagny.*

ABOVE *A shot which captures the heat and confusion of battle shows British infantry preparing to advance near Cagny on the second day of Goodwood.*

49

OPERATION COBRA

Tuesday
25
JULY
D+49

Monday
31
JULY
D+55

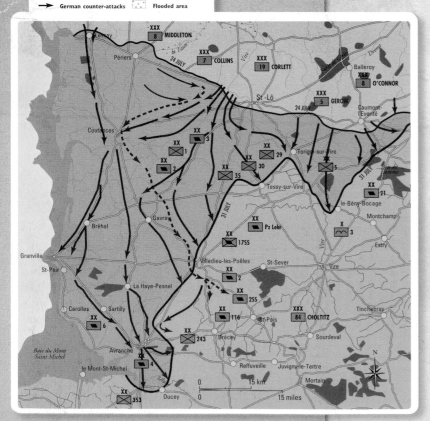

OPERATION COBRA AND THE BREAKOUT 25–31 JULY 1944

Front line 24 July	German retreats
Front line 31 July	Sandy shoreline
US advance movements	Rocks
German counter-attacks	Flooded area

US 4TH ARMOURED DIVISION

On 5 July Eisenhower observed that three factors were making life hard for the Americans: German fighting quality, the nature of the country, and the weather. By the time they took St-Lô the Americans had learnt a good deal about bocage fighting, and if they were well aware of how unpleasant this was for them, they underestimated the damage that they were doing to the Germans. On 13 July Kluge, who arrived in Normandy full of enthusiasm, warned Hitler's staff that his infantry was worn perilously thin. He needed more tanks "to act as corset stays behind the troops." The situation was now "very serious. ... If a hole breaks open, I have to patch it."

Eisenhower was disappointed by Goodwood, and affirmed that he was "pinning our immediate hopes on Bradley's attack." Montgomery, meanwhile, ordered Dempsey to "fatten up" his operations in order to ensure that the Germans could not swing to meet the forthcoming attack, Operation Cobra. The original Cobra plan was modest, and envisaged an attack southwards to Coutances and then a jab westwards, to cut off the defenders of the coastal strip, and leave the US First Army consolidating on the line Coutances-Caumont, ready to exploit further. The key breakthrough was to be made by VII Corps, tightly concentrated just west of St-Lô, and before the attack German positions were to be saturated by heavy bombers. General Collins' infantry would attack after the bombing, and once they had created a gap in the defences his armoured divisions would roll on through.

The bombing was dogged by misfortune. Although the attack was postponed because of bad weather on 24 July some bombers struck anyway, and several Americans were killed or wounded. On the following day the bombers came again, and this time 111 Americans were killed and another 490 wounded. Although the bombing had clearly rattled the defence, the initial infantry attacks still ran into firm resistance. However,

General Collins believed that the Germans were shaken enough for him to commit his armour, and though the situation on 26 July "did not appear too bright" he did just that. Collins' instincts were correct, and by the end of the day one of his divisional commanders exulted: "This thing has busted wide open." There was indeed a jagged breach in the German defences, and Kluge had too little armour to counter-attack.

Bradley's success lay as much in what followed Cobra as in the battle itself. Recognizing that the Germans could no longer furnish a cohesive defence, on 28 July he issued orders for exploitation of the initial breakthrough. The results were impressive. The Americans reached Avranches on 30 July, and on the following day they seized the little bridge over the River Sélune at Pontaubault just before the Germans arrived to destroy it. Kluge admitted that "It's a madhouse here," and acknowledged that his whole left flank had collapsed.

On 1 August, with tanks of 4th Armoured Division rattling past Pontaubault towards Brittany, the Americans activated their new command structure, with Bradley stepping up to command 12th Army Group, Lieutenant General Courtney H. Hodges taking over First Army and Lieutenant General George S. Patton assuming command of the newly-formed US Third Army. Eisenhower declared that Montgomery would remain ground force commander until SHAEF arrived in France and he assumed personal command. Although there was still much hard fighting to be done, Cobra had changed the pattern of the campaign.

RIGHT *American infantry and tank destroyers west of St-Lô.*

BELOW *Smoke rising from the "bombing box", just south of the St-Lô–Périers road, as heavy bombers prepare the way for Cobra, 25 July.*

"IT WAS HELL. ...
The planes **KEPT COMING** overhead like a **CONVEYOR** BELT, and the **BOMB CARPETS** came down, now ahead, now on the right, now on the left. ... **"**

LIEUTENANT GENERAL FRITZ BAYERLEIN,
PANZER LEHR DIVISION

GEORGE S. PATTON *came from a well-to-do family with military traditions. Commissioned in 1909, he commanded a tank brigade in France in 1918 with great success. He led an armoured division in 1941 and was an army commander in 1943, but was shelved after slapping two shell-shocked soldiers. Patton commanded Third Army in its dash across France in 1944, but mismanaged the campaign to take Metz. Flamboyant, profane, gifted but flawed, Patton died after a car crash in 1945.*

US THIRD ARMY

RIGHT *A US Sherman tank with the modification to its hull. These "horns" enabled the tank to rip its way through the hedges-on-banks, so typical of the bocage.*

ABOVE *An American column of jeeps and trucks advancing on Coutances through a badly damaged village following a fierce bombardment.*

51

OPERATION LUTTICH

ABOVE *The Panther tank, with a 75mm gun, was developed by the Germans to counter the threat posed by the Soviet T-34. The Americans and British first encountered it in significant numbers in Normandy.*

Hitler persistently intervened in the conduct of military operations. Sometimes he was right: his decision to stand fast in the face of the Russian counter-attack in December 1941, for instance, was well judged. But by August 1944 his grip on reality had been severely eroded, and the unsuccessful assassination attempt of 20 July had increased his paranoia towards the General Staff. The decision to mount Operation Lüttich, the Mortain counter-attack, was his. On the face of things it was not wholly foolish. Exploitation after Cobra had left the Americans with a narrow corridor between Mortain and the coast, and it was not inconceivable that this could be cut, leaving Patton's divisions to the south dangerously short of fuel and supplies. But while Kluge and his staff recognized that a counter-attack could buy time, perhaps enough to fall back to a new defence line, Hitler envisaged something wholly different: a massive counter-stroke which would reverse his fortunes in the west and, as he put it, throw the Allies into the sea.

The Mortain counter-attack laboured under many disadvantages: several senior German commanders were markedly lacking in enthusiasm, and most participating units were already under-strength. However, in one respect Hitler's luck held. The weather on 7 August, when the battle began, was poor, grounding Allied fighter-bombers. And if Bradley had brief warning of the attack, produced by Ultra, for some units on the ground the sudden appearance of numerous determined Germans came as a very unpleasant shock. Mortain itself had only just been occupied by the veteran US 30th Division, and although it was driven out of the town, the dominant Hill 317, just to the east, was held by part of an infantry battalion with artillery observers in "one of the outstanding small unit achievements in the course of the campaign." When the weather cleared the observers were able to direct fire onto the main road to the coast, just below them, and USAAF Thunderbolts and RAF Typhoons arrived to lacerate the attackers. Despite there being some early progress, the attack was going nowhere.

Hitler remained convinced that the offensive could have succeeded if it had been heavier, and ordered Eberbach, removed from command of 5th Panzer Army and given a scratch headquarters specifically for the new attack, to try again on 11 August. Eberbach soon recognized that he had too few tanks for the task, and Allied air superiority meant that they could only move while early-morning mist grounded aircraft. And Kluge could see that things were coming unstitched elsewhere: the Canadians were pushing hard down the Caen-Falaise road, and further south the Americans were cutting up from Le Mans towards Alençon. By continuing to strike westwards, the Germans were putting their heads further into the noose, and on 11 August Hitler authorized Eberbach to disengage, although, hopelessly unrealistically, he still hoped to try again later.

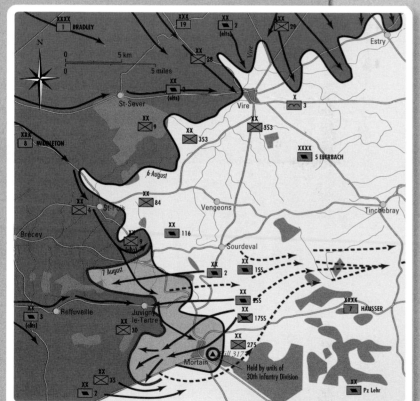

OPERATION LUTTICH

7–8 AUGUST 1944

→ US advance movements
— Front line 6 August
➡ German attacks 7 August
— Front line 7 August
-→ German retreat 8 August

US 30TH DIVISION

52

GUNTHER VON KLUGE *was an army commander from 1939–40, and promoted to field marshal after victory in France. Injured in Russia in 1943, he was re-employed in 1944 as Commander in Chief West, replacing Rundstedt on 3 July. Initially full of enthusiasm, he speedily concluded that his position was hopeless. Ordered to Germany in the wake of the 20 July assassination plot, he took poison on 19 August. His last letter spoke of shame at his failure but of continuing loyalty to Hitler.*

"TANKS are the backbone of OUR DEFENCE, when they are withdrawn, our front will give way. If, as I foresee, this plan does not succeed, CATASTROPHE is INEVITABLE."

FIELD MARSHAL GUNTHER VON KLUGE, COMMANDER IN CHIEF WEST

LARGE PHOTOGRAPH *The danger of road moved in daylight. This German convoy has been strafed by USAAF Thunderbolts.*

INSET RIGHT *Soft-skinned vehicles were hideously vulnerable to attack from the air.*

LEFT *A company of Tiger II tanks, part of an SS Panzer division, camouflaged near Mortain on the eve of Operation Lüttich.*

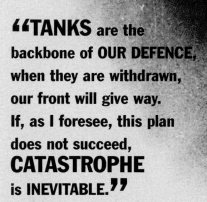

TACTICAL AIR SUPPORT

The Allies enjoyed air superiority throughout the campaign. The Luftwaffe had been weakened before D-Day by losses in combat and the effects of bombing on the German industrial base. Indeed, the erosion of the Luftwaffe's fighter strength was one of the by-products of the strategic bombing campaign. It became harder to train pilots, and by 1944 German air power was in a descending spiral which could have only one result. German soldiers lived with the constant threat of air attack: they joked darkly that the "Normandy look" was an upward stare that gave a man a crick in his neck, and photographs and newsreels reveal constant emphasis on camouflage.

Yet if air power made a crucial contribution to Allied victory, it was not decisive in itself. Armies and air forces were not always comfortable bedfellows. The "bomber barons", like Carl Spaatz and Ira Eaker in the USAAF and Arthur Harris in the RAF, believed that their heavy bombers should be used against strategic targets in Germany, not tactical targets in Normandy, and the experience of Goodwood and Cobra confirmed them in this view. Even at a lower level, where air power was tactical in function, its effectiveness was limited by personality clashes. Air Marshal Coningham of Second Tactical Air Force cordially detested Montgomery, and Tedder, Eisenhower's deputy, sympathized

with him. In contrast, Air Vice Marshal Harry Broadhurst, who supported Dempsey's Second Army, got on well with soldiers. So too did USAAF Major General Elwood R. "Pete" Quesada, whose IX Tactical Air Command supported Bradley. He not only enjoyed an excellent working relationship with Bradley himself, but persuaded him to put aircraft radios into tanks to improve communication between ground and air.

Communication was itself a major difficulty, and one of the reasons why Goodwood made limited progress was that the one forward air controller on the main axis of the advance was in an unarmoured vehicle which was knocked out early on. It was rarely enough to target air attacks on a particular area: pilots had a better chance of success if a forward air controller could give them last minute directions, perhaps with a smoke shell to mark the target. Next, the limitations of the weapons in use limited the effectiveness of air attacks. Infantry and soft-skinned vehicles could be dealt with by machine-gun or cannon fire, but tanks were harder to destroy, and rockets, like those used by RAF Typhoons, lacked accuracy when used against moving armour. Even when the skies cleared over Mortain, and the flail of Allied air power was applied relentlessly, more tanks were abandoned by their terrified crews than were actually destroyed by rockets. Bad weather often made flying impossible, and "loiter time" over the battlefield was all too short until sufficient aircraft were based on temporary airstrips in France.

Lastly, the Germans were adept at generating comprehensive ground-based air defence, with 88mm guns

ABOVE *Marauder medium bombers of the US 9th Air Force attacking German units moving up to the battlefront by road.*

ELWOOD R. "PETE" QUESADA *had a good range of staff and flying appointments before the war began. He went to North Africa at the head of XII Fighter Command, and was a natural choice for promotion to major general to lead IX Tactical Air Command. He landed near Omaha on D+1, and his airmen opened the first landing strip in France that day. He worked closely with Bradley to orchestrate effective air support in Normandy, and during the German Ardennes offensive.*

RIGHT *A rocket-armed RAF Typhoon taking off from a forward airstrip. Aircraft were refueled and rearmed on these strips, enjoying longer "loiter time" over the battlefield than if they had to return to Britain after each mission.*

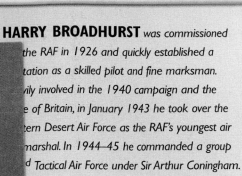

HARRY BROADHURST was commissioned
~~the~~ RAF in 1926 and quickly established a
~~repu~~tation as a skilled pilot and fine marksman.
~~Heav~~ily involved in the 1940 campaign and the
~~Battle~~ of Britain, in January 1943 he took over the
~~Wes~~tern Desert Air Force as the RAF's youngest air
~~vice marshal. In 1944–45 he commanded a group
~~in 2n~~d Tactical Air Force under Sir Arthur Coningham.
~~He en~~joyed Montgomery's confidence, and worked well with him during the campaign.

reaching up for high-flying aircraft and lighter weapons taking
a toll of lower targets. Second Tactical Air Force and
UK-based Fighter Command units between them lost 829
aircraft and over 1,000 aircrew killed or missing, and for the
campaign as a whole the USAAF lost an average of 34 men
and eight aircraft, and the RAF 36 men and nine aircraft, for
every thousand sorties. There were times when the efforts
of Allied pilots were not appreciated by men slogging it out
on the ground, but the skies over Normandy were anything
but safe.

ATTACHMENT

The logbook of a British Typhoon
pilot, Flying Officer Henry "Poppa"
Ambrose of 175 Squadron (whose
motto was "Stop at Nothing"),
detailing his ground-support sorties
from 8 to 31 August 1944.

LEFT Canadians pause on their
way to Falaise as Allied bombs fall
just ahead of them.

OPERATIONS TOTALIZE & TRACTAB

GUY SIMONDS was commissioned into the Canadian permanent force between the wars, and was Chief of Staff of I Canadian Corps before taking command of 1st Canadian Infantry Division in Sicily. He led II Canadian Corps in Normandy, and after the war became Chief Instructor of the Imperial Defence College, Commandant of the Canadian National Defence College and finally Chief of the Canadian General Staff. Simonds was temperamental, but set high standards, and was one of the best Allied corps commanders.

BELOW Canadian infantry in half-tracks advance on Falaise. The white star on the vehicles was an Allied recognition symbol.

In the wake of Goodwood, Lieutenant General Guy Simonds' II Canadian Corps assumed responsibility for the offensive towards Falaise, and in the process landed two heavy blows on the Germans, Operation Totalize on 7–10 August and Tractable on 14–16 August. Although the rolling countryside crossed by the Caen-Falaise road was well suited to defence based on the long reach of the 88mm gun, Simonds planned to minimize its effectiveness by attacking with infantry at night, pushing armour through once the defence was breached. Heavy bombers would support the attacks, and artillery, which had grown in strength and effect as the campaign had developed, would crash out ahead of the advancing troops.

One of the lessons of Goodwood was that unprotected infantry found it hard to co-operate effectively with tanks in open country. Simonds accordingly decided to put much of his infantry into extemporized armoured personnel carriers, from which they would dismount only to attack their objectives. These vehicles were created by removing the guns, seats and ammunition bins from Priest self-propelled guns. Steel sheets were welded across the openings, and as armour plate was in short supply it was improvised by putting a thin layer of sand between sheets of mild steel. The new vehicles were known as "holy rollers" or "unfrocked priests." To help the armoured columns, moving in tight formation on the axis of the main road, keep their direction in the dark, there were to be navigational aids like light anti-aircraft guns firing tracer ammunition in the direction of advance and radio direction beams.

Simonds' corps, comprising 2nd and 3rd Canadian Infantry Divisions, 4th Canadian Armoured Division and 2nd Canadian Armoured Brigade, was reinforced by the British 51st Highland Division and 33rd Armoured Brigade, and by 1st Polish Armoured Division. The [...] support for Tractable be[...] 11.00 on the night of 7 A[...] the attacking columns mo[...] forward shortly afterwar[...] were useful gains during [...] and after dawn Polish an[...] tanks moved through the [...] getting as far as Cintheau[...] advance of six or seven [...] Subsequent progress, aga[...] impressive, and the atta[...] Tractable followed a sim[...] were in daylight, with me[...] on the morning of 14 A[...] afternoon. The attacker[...] Laizon, and despite som[...] predictably stiff resistan[...] infantry of 2nd Canadia[...] only did Totalize and Tra[...] important objective, but[...] plans for an offensive ag[...] wonder that Hitler adm[...] day of his life.

CANADIAN 2ND ARMOURED BRIGADE

RIGHT Heat and dust: infantry moving up for Operation Totalize.

LEFT Smoke and debris rising from a German ammunition dump hit by an air attack north of Falaise in mid-July.

HARRY BROADHURST was commissioned into the RAF in 1926 and quickly established a reputation as a skilled pilot and fine marksman. Heavily involved in the 1940 campaign and the Battle of Britain, in January 1943 he took over the Western Desert Air Force as the RAF's youngest air vice marshal. In 1944–45 he commanded a group in 2nd Tactical Air Force under Sir Arthur Coningham. He enjoyed Montgomery's confidence, and worked well with him during the campaign.

reaching up for high-flying aircraft and lighter weapons taking a toll of lower targets. Second Tactical Air Force and UK-based Fighter Command units between them lost 829 aircraft and over 1,000 aircrew killed or missing, and for the campaign as a whole the USAAF lost an average of 34 men and eight aircraft, and the RAF 36 men and nine aircraft, for every thousand sorties. There were times when the efforts of Allied pilots were not appreciated by men slogging it out on the ground, but the skies over Normandy were anything but safe.

ATTACHMENT

The logbook of a British Typhoon pilot, Flying Officer Henry "Poppa" Ambrose of 175 Squadron (whose motto was "Stop at Nothing"), detailing his ground-support sorties from 8 to 31 August 1944.

LEFT Canadians pause on their way to Falaise as Allied bombs fall just ahead of them.

OPERATIONS TOTALIZE & TRACTABLE

Monday
7
AUGUST
D+62

Wednesday
16
AUGUST
D+71

GUY SIMONDS *was commissioned into the Canadian permanent force between the wars, and was Chief of Staff of I Canadian Corps before taking command of 1st Canadian Infantry Division in Sicily. He led II Canadian Corps in Normandy, and after the war became Chief Instructor of the Imperial Defence College, Commandant of the Canadian National Defence College and finally Chief of the Canadian General Staff. Simonds was temperamental, but set high standards, and was one of the best Allied corps commanders.*

BELOW *Canadian infantry in half-tracks advance on Falaise. The white star on the vehicles was an Allied recognition symbol.*

In the wake of Goodwood, Lieutenant General Guy Simonds' II Canadian Corps assumed responsibility for the offensive towards Falaise, and in the process landed two heavy blows on the Germans, Operation Totalize on 7–10 August and Tractable on 14–16 August. Although the rolling countryside crossed by the Caen-Falaise road was well suited to defence based on the long reach of the 88mm gun, Simonds planned to minimize its effectiveness by attacking with infantry at night, pushing armour through once the defence was breached. Heavy bombers would support the attacks, and artillery, which had grown in strength and effect as the campaign had developed, would crash out ahead of the advancing troops.

One of the lessons of Goodwood was that unprotected infantry found it hard to co-operate effectively with tanks in open country. Simonds accordingly decided to put much of his infantry into extemporized armoured personnel carriers, from which they would dismount only to attack their objectives. These vehicles were created by removing the guns, seats and ammunition bins from Priest self-propelled guns. Steel sheets were welded across the openings, and as armour plate was in short supply it was improvised by putting a thin layer of sand between sheets of mild steel. The new vehicles were known as "holy rollers" or "unfrocked priests." To help the armoured columns, moving in tight formation on the axis of the main road, keep their direction in the dark, there were to be navigational aids like light anti-aircraft guns firing tracer ammunition in the direction of advance and radio direction beams.

Simonds' corps, comprising 2nd and 3rd Canadian Infantry Divisions, 4th Canadian Armoured Division and 2nd Canadian Armoured Brigade, was reinforced by the British 51st Highland Division and 33rd Armoured Brigade, and by 1st Polish Armoured Division. The bombing support for Tractable began at 11.00 on the night of 7 August, and the attacking columns moved forward shortly afterwards. There were useful gains during the night, and after dawn Polish and Canadian tanks moved through the infantry, getting as far as Cintheaux, a total advance of six or seven miles.

Subsequent progress, against a hardening defence, was less impressive, and the attack paused on 10 June. Operation Tractable followed a similar pattern, though the first attacks were in daylight, with medium bombers going in at 11.30 on the morning of 14 August and heavies following in the afternoon. The attackers were soon across the little River Laizon, and despite some inaccurate bombing and predictably stiff resistance, by midnight on 16 August the infantry of 2nd Canadian Division had taken Falaise. Not only did Totalize and Tractable result in the capture of this important objective, but they helped disorganize German plans for an offensive against the Americans. It was small wonder that Hitler admitted that 15 August was the worst day of his life.

BRITISH 51ST HIGHLAND INFANTRY DIVISION

CANADIAN 2ND ARMOURED BRIGADE

RIGHT *Heat and dust: infantry moving up for Operation Totalize.*

OPERATIONS TOTALIZE & TRACTABLE 7–15 AUGUST 1944

— Front line 7 August
— Front line 11 August
— Front line 15 August
— German defence zone
* Night bomber targets 7 August
* Day bomber targets 8 August
✳ Saturation bombing prior to attack

LEFT *Canadian infantry clearing a village on the way to Falaise. The second soldier is a sniper.*

BELOW *Canadians pass destroyed vehicles on the Caen-Falaise road.*

KURT "PANZER" MEYER, *whose Nazi Party membership book appears above, joined the SS in 1933, and fought in Poland before earning the Knight's Cross in Crete in 1941. In 1944, at the age of 33, he commanded the 12th SS Panzer Division Hitlerjugend in the Caen sector. He was a tough and resolute man. Driving up the Caen-Falaise road at the beginning of Operation Totalize he found infantry streaming back in panic. He stood in the middle of the road and rallied them, ensuring that their positions around Cintheaux were held. After the war a Canadian tribunal sentenced him to death for the murder of prisoners. The sentence was commuted, and he was released in 1954, dying shortly afterwards.*

THE FALAISE POCKET

The battle of the Falaise Pocket was improvised in response to Allied successes and German failure. Both Montgomery and Bradley were quick to spot the chance offered them. Bradley told the visiting Henry Morgenthau, US Treasury Secretary, that: "This is an opportunity that comes to a commander not more than once in a century. We are about to destroy an entire German army." The Allies had two major options, a "short hook" to create a pocket near Falaise, or a "long hook" to the Seine to achieve greater encirclement. Both were more difficult and more risky than they appear in hindsight, for an unplanned envelopment by two national army groups presented extraordinary problems of co-ordination. Moreover, though the German army was indeed beaten, some of its components still displayed their old aggressiveness, and

were to show every determination of breaking any Allied ring at its weakest point.

A telephone conversation between Bradley and Montgomery on 8 August established the short hook as the preferred option: Bradley's men would jab north towards Argentan, forming the lower jaw of a vice which would meet the British and Canadians jaw crunching down from Caen. Bradley halted his leading corps, Third Army's XV, just south of Argentan on 13 August, arguing that it was "better to have a solid shoulder at Argentan than a broken neck at Falaise." He was across the boundary into 21st Army Group's area, Eberbach's armour was still threatening, and he was uncertain whether there were enough Germans in the Pocket to make the operation worthwhile. Bradley later complained that Montgomery's caution delayed closing the gap, but it is fair to say that neither commander (nor indeed Eisenhower himself) displayed that killer instinct which would have enabled them to close the gap sooner. Nor ought we to be

Sunday
13
AUGUST
D+68

Monday
21
AUGUST
D+76

US XV CORPS

"Forty-eight hours after the CLOSING OF THE GAP I was conducted through it on foot, to encounter SCENES that could only be described by DANTE. It was literally possible to walk for hundreds of yards at a time, stepping on nothing but DEAD AND DECAYING FLESH."

GENERAL DWIGHT D. EISENHOWER

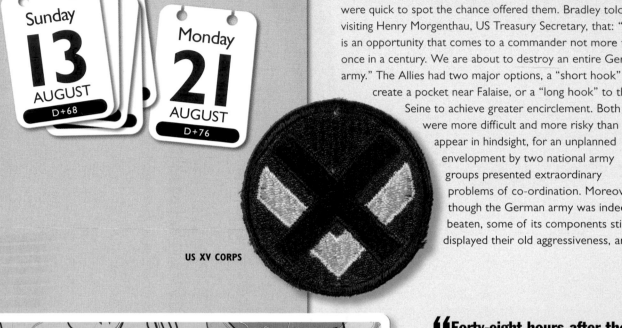

FALAISE POCKET
6–19 AUGUST 1944

— Front line 6 August
— Front line 16 August
— Front line 19 August

ABOVE *Canadian tanks closing in on the Falaise pocket. A flail tank, equipped with rotating chains to explode mines, is on the left.*

surprised. These were the armies of mighty democracies nearing the end of a long war, with a chain of command which reflected national and personal tensions.

Early on 16 August Kluge recommended evacuation of the salient, and had begun to withdraw before formal permission reached him later that day. It was his last act as a commander, for Field Marshal Walther Model arrived to relieve him on 17 August. As the Germans began to pull back, Bradley, following a phone conversation with Montgomery, ordered Patton to seize Chambois: the jaws of the vice were inching shut. By the evening of 18 August there was still a gap of three miles between the Americans and the Polish armoured division, on the extreme south-east edge of Mongomery's thrust, but on 19 August Americans and Poles met in Chambois. There was still some very sharp fighting. Major David Currie of the South Alberta Regiment earned the Victoria Cross in St-Lambert-sur-Dives, and the Poles, on what they called "The Mace" above Chambois, fought

POLISH ARMOURED 1ST DIVISION

desperately to keep Germans in the Pocket and to prevent units outside from boring an escape hole.

When the battle ended on 21 August the killing fields of the Pocket, repeatedly strafed by Allied aircraft, resembled, as Eisenhower put it, something out of Dante's Inferno, where it was difficult to walk without treading on human flesh. Although, as subsequent critics pointed out, greater destruction could have been wrought had the Pocket been sealed sooner, it was the culmination of a defeat of shocking proportions. In the previous ten weeks the defenders of Normandy had lost some 1,300 tanks, at least 50,000 dead, and 200,000 prisoners.

RIGHT *The debris of defeat near Chambois in the Falaise Pocket. Not all the dead in the Pocket were combatants. Chambois alone lost 17 inhabitants.*

BELOW *German transport destroyed by artillery fire. Many combatants found the numerous dead horses in the Pocket particularly depressing.*

DAVID CURRIE *was a Saskatchewan mechanic before joining the Canadian army. Commissioned from the ranks, by July 1944 he was commanding a squadron of the 29th Canadian Armoured Reconnaissance Regiment (South Alberta Regiment). In August he took St-Lambert-sur-Dives, on a German withdrawal route through the Falaise Pocket, and held it in the face of fierce attacks, earning the first Canadian VC of the campaign. He survived the war, and later became sergeant at arms in the Canadian parliament.*

ENCLOSURES

1 *A 50-franc note, printed in the United States and issued to Allied troops for use in France.*

2 *Aerial leaflet dropped by the Allies on German troops to facilitate their safe surrender.*

3 *A page from the official war diary of the 10th Brigade of the 1st Polish Armoured Division detailing its action in closing the Falaise Gap on 20 August. See translation on page 63.*

BELOW *Germans captured near Falaise, relief evident on many of their faces, pass a column of Canadian tanks moving up to the front.*

THE LIBERATION OF PARIS

Saturday **19** AUGUST D+74

Friday **25** AUGUST D+80

The Americans struck out for the Seine before fighting had finished at Falaise. On 19 August they crossed the river near Mantes, and the British crossed at Vernon five days later. Hitler still hoped to hold Paris, but Model pointed out that the city's retention would be "a big military problem" and knew that there was little chance of holding it with the forces at his disposal.

The Paris Resistance had views of its own. Although de Gaulle sent an emissary with instructions to avoid any "premature rising", on 19 August policemen hoisted the tricouleur above the Prefecture of Police, and there was soon sporadic fighting. The military commander of Paris, Lieutenant General Dietrich von Choltitz, planned to defend the southern and western suburbs, but was told to prepare for demolition the city's public utilities, bridges and many of its most famous buildings. Choltitz was an honourable man with no appetite for this, but had a family in Germany and needed to find a solution that would neither destroy Paris nor result in "premature" surrender.

On 20 August Choltitz agreed to a short-lived truce, and a flurry of Resistance emissaries to the Allies resulted in Eisenhower's agreement that the Free French 2nd Armoured Division under Major General Philippe Leclerc, which had arrived in France on 1 August, would drive straight for Paris. When Leclerc received the order his men were still 120 miles away, but he reached Rambouillet, where he met de Gaulle, on 23 August. They agreed that Leclerc should edge eastwards to find the least-defended route into the city, and at 9.30 on the evening of 24 August his three leading tanks drew up outside the Town Hall. On the next day there was a last burst of fighting, with moments of terrible poignancy as French soldiers died

close to home, before Choltitz surrendered. On 26 August Charles de Gaulle walked ahead of his generals and a great crowd for a *Te Deum* at Notre Dame. There was sniping on the way, but his step never faltered.

As Paris revelled in its liberation the Allied armies hurtled across France. On 1 September Eisenhower assumed command of ground forces, but for the moment he had little impact as his divisions rolled across the battlefields of the First World War, and over the Marne and the Somme, on which Hitler briefly hoped to make a stand. The German divisions which had escaped from Normandy were still too badly bruised to fight. Although those of Army Group G, dislodged by an Allied invasion of the Riviera on 15 August, were in better shape, even Walther Model, "Führer's Fireman" though he was, could not make a stand till he neared the borders of Germany.

Montgomery had always thought in terms of crossing the Seine in D+90 days, and had indeed achieved it. He was wrong to maintain that things had gone according to plan: few campaigns do, and that in Normandy was no exception. It is unfortunate that the tensions inherent in the alliance were magnified as leaders wrote their memoirs and attracted biographers. The real truth of Normandy was that the forces of a mighty coalition had entered the continent of Europe and, mistakes notwithstanding, struck a telling blow at its occupiers. They deserve our gratitude.

PHILIPPE LECLERC

was wounded and captured in 1940. He escaped and joined de Gaulle in Britain, was sent to equatorial Africa (with a nom de guerre to protect his family), and led a column across the Sahara to join the British 8th Army in Libya. He commanded 2nd Armoured Division, the first Allied unit to enter Paris, in 1944–45, and was French representative at the Japanese surrender. Killed in a 1947 plane crash, Leclerc was posthumously created Marshal of France.

ABOVE LEFT *A Frenchwoman exults as the tricouleur is raised in Paris.*

RIGHT *A US tank destroyer crosses the Seine by means of a pontoon bridge built by American engineers.*

LEFT *Battle in the shadow of the Arc de Triomphe. Soldiers of the French 2nd Armoured Division look out across German dead on the Champs Elysées.*

BELOW *Germans are led into captivity by an escort more necessary to deter assault than to prevent escape.*

BOTTOM *Brothers reunited. A policeman, in steel helmet, greets his brother, a member of 2nd Armoured Division, in newly liberated Paris on 25 August.*

BELOW *Parisians extend welcoming hands to US troops entering the city on 25 August.*

THE LIBERATION OF PARIS

14–25 AUGUST 1944

Front line 14 August
Front line 19 August
Front line 25 August

English Channel

Abbeville · Dieppe · Amiens · St-Quentin · Laon · Reims
XXXX 15 SALMUTH
XXXX 7 HAUSSER · Remnants
Le Havre · Rouen · Beauvais · Compiègne · Soissons
XXXXX 21 MONTGOMERY
XXX XXXX EBERBACH · Remnants
XXXXX 8 MODEL
XXXX 1 CRERAR · Caen · Lisieux · XXX 1 · Louviers · Vernon · Pontoise · Château-Thierry
XXXX 2 DEMPSEY · Falaise · XXX 2 · XXX 30 · Évreux · PARIS
Mortain · Domfront · Argentan · XXX 7 · Dreux · XXX 2 Fr. · XXX 1 CHEVALLARIE · Melun · Seine
XXXX HODGES · Alençon · Chartres · Fontainebleau · Romilly · Troyes
Mayenne · XXX · Pithiviers · Sens · XXX 4
XXXX PATTON · Angers · le Mans · Châteaudun · Orléans · Montargis
XXXX BRADLEY · XXX · Saumur · Tours · Vierzon

0   50 km
0   50 miles

N

INDEX

Page numbers in *italic* refer to picture captions